Social Media Marketing 2019

30 Powerful Strategies to Become an Influencer for Billions of People on Facebook, Instagram, YouTube, LinkedIn and Others. Great to Listen in a Car!

© **Copyright by Mark Graham 2019 - All rights reserved.**

The content contained within this book may not be reproduced, duplicated or transmitted without direct written permission from the author or the publisher.

Under no circumstances will any blame or legal responsibility be held against the publisher, or author, for any damages, reparation, or monetary loss due to the information contained within this book. Either directly or indirectly.

Legal Notice:

This book is copyright protected. This book is only for personal use. You cannot amend, distribute, sell, use, quote or paraphrase any part, or the content within this book, without the consent of the author or publisher.

Disclaimer Notice:

Please note the information contained within this document is for educational and entertainment purposes only. All effort has been executed to present accurate, up to date, and reliable, complete information. No warranties of any kind are declared or implied. Readers acknowledge that the author is not engaging in the rendering of legal, financial, medical or professional advice. The content within this book has been derived from various sources. Please consult a licensed professional before attempting any techniques outlined in this book.

By reading this document, the reader agrees that under no circumstances is the author responsible for any losses, direct or indirect, which are incurred as a result of the use of information contained within this document, including, but not limited to, — errors, omissions, or inaccuracies.

Table of Contents

Introduction..5
Chapter One: Instagram..............................7
Chapter Two: Facebook.............................16
Chapter Three: LinkedIn...........................70
Chapter Four: YouTube.............................93
Conclusion...147
References..148

Introduction

In the current economy, the best way to sell your products is by reaching out to people through a medium that ensures memorability. Social media in 2019 is not just used to connect with friends and to share memes, but is also a way through which people decide what they like and what they want to buy. Instagram influencers and Facebook Pages constantly determine which products and brands sell and which don't. The best part about social media is that it's cheap and doesn't require too much of an effort. You can create a brand for your product from the comfort of your home, reaching billions of people around the world.

The only thing social media requires is acute attention to detail, especially when it comes to selling your brand. You won't get famous simply by making a post about your product — you have to catch people's attention. That in itself is a herculean task, but once you do, you will reap the numerous gains that come with social media fame.

The purpose of social media marketing is not to compete with brands that are global and have millions of followers. All you have to do is find a niche audience for your brand; people who want something authentic, a brand that is not only approachable but takes feedback from its users. The one thing that big brands can never offer is a personal connection with their numerous consumers. Through social media, you can create a dedicated following for your brand, and all you have to do is use the tricks given in this book.

Through these chapters, we will break down the most famous social media websites of 2019, and how you can use them to reach out to your audience. You will learn about the basics of how these websites function, the various features they have, some tricks and tips to gain competitive advantage, and ways to actually make some money from these sites.

Chapter One: Instagram

Instagram is a terrific platform for building your brand. This is especially true for certain ecommerce niches like fashion and lifestyle, but not so much for others, which is why we will keep the discussion on Instagram short. Service-based brands cannot always be portrayed as effectively as products on Instagram. On the other hand, if you're building an e-commerce-based brand, then this chapter will be vital to your social media marketing efforts to showcase your brand and wow hundreds of thousands of people.

Instagram is a visual platform, so the stories and content that you will be preparing for Instagram have to be highly image-based by nature. Instagram is chock full of online shoppers who are looking for a more streamlined newsfeed based on images rather than Facebook; this is a fact that most e-commerce businesses utilize to their full advantage. Instagram also boasts a higher audience engagement rate than Facebook, which is another big plus for social media marketing in 2019. Combining the engagement rates with the fact that most of Instagram's audience is actively looking to buy something, successful marketing campaigns on the platform can and will lead to substantially higher conversion rates in sales numbers for your brand than Facebook. The only problem is that, while Facebook's algorithm can be somewhat predictable, Instagram's is a lot like Google — unpredictable and ever-changing based on factors that move up and down with each algorithm update.

Strategies for Instagram Marketing

To run successful social media marketing campaigns on Instagram, here are a few things that you should keep in mind:

Update New Posts

Frequently update with new posts so your brand presence doesn't get pushed back by others. This means constantly creating new image-based content for your brand's newsfeed. Like Google and Facebook, Instagram also employs machine learning and AI to streamline your audience's newsfeed, so make sure your posts share relevant themes to appear constantly.

Use Images And Videos

Videos are also an important part of Instagram now, especially stories. The video duration for Instagram stories are very short, so it's best that you create a storyboard to make a structured narrative for your stories. If you have a minimum following of 10,000 people on Instagram, don't forget to add links to your stories. When Instagram stories were first launched, only big brands could add links to story posts, but now any brand entity with the above-mentioned following can add website links to stories, increasing the chance of driving traffic to your website for sales conversions.

Create Viable Marketing Strategies

Introduce viable marketing strategies that will encourage your Instagram followers to tag you in their stories. This will ensure that you constantly stay on their newsfeed, as well. On the flip side, you should also publish user-generated content that is relevant to the theme of your brand to gain bigger outreach. Unlike Facebook and Webmaster outreach methods, which require good communication skills to make the other party agree to share your posts and content, this happens naturally. Additionally, your audience feels special, making this a great technique for an increased audience outreach that is gained organically (without any paid promotion).

Use Social Influencers

Don't underestimate the power of influencers on

Instagram, as they are the segment of the Instagram population that keeps the social media marketing ball rolling. To run successful social media marketing campaigns on Instagram, you need to have the best and most followed influencers within your reach. Now, there's one catch to this — hiring influencers to promote your brand can be very expensive, so you'd better have a fat wad of cash in order to hire one. Alternatively, you can provide them with free products from your brand in exchange for showcasing them, which is a tactic that works well with influencers who have a small or medium audience reach. Bigger brands often offer perks like paid vacations and photo-shoots, which can also bring down payments made to influencers. When choosing influencers, pick the ones who showcase their daily lifestyle while promoting brands, since they come off as more genuine, in turn, making the audience feel that the brand represents their regular lifestyle. Different types of influencers are suited for different kinds of promotions. An influencer specializing in luxury brands will not be effective for your marketing campaign if you're promoting non-luxury products that can be termed as average.

Show Your Instagram

Since SEO for Instagram is a bad idea in general, one thing you can do is show your brand's Instagram profile on a search engine by using Google's schema.org markup. Not only should you do this for

Instagram, but you should use it for all other social media profiles of your brand on other platforms, as well, such as Facebook, Twitter, and LinkedIn.

Provide a Rich Bio

Providing a rich bio for your Instagram profile is crucial for audience outreach. The bio has to be written with as much care as meta-descriptions for your website (which will be discussed in the last chapter). Include the core keywords you have chosen for your search engine rankings in the same way you would for meta-descriptions. The bio is the only HTML-rendered element on Instagram that can be crawled by search engine bots, so this is the only valid SEO optimization you can do for your Instagram profile. Also, don't forget to add a link to the main website on your Instagram profile, though it comes with a no-follow tag by default — something is better than nothing, right? You should also add email addresses, as this has started to become standard practice when setting up Instagram profiles.

Focus On Your Profile Design

Focus on your profile design when setting up your account. Unlike Facebook, where you can have different types of content to keep the audience engaged, Instagram is all about looking good. If your profile doesn't look good, then don't expect high levels of audience engagement in your marketing efforts. Your image content should have a consistent design and editing style that will make it stand out from other brands.

Use Instagram Stories

If you can afford it, cover your brand's launch via carousels and Instagram stories. Carousels allow you to place multiple pictures one after another to form a structured narrative without appearing spammy.

Use Instagram LiveStream

Similar to Facebook's live-video streaming option, Instagram also added a similar attribute last year as one of its platform features, though it has mostly gone unnoticed by many small- and medium-scale brands. If you're confident that you can create an attractive LiveStream event, go ahead and do so — you will be capitalizing on something most businesses aren't. While you're at it, you can also invite influencers to take part in your live broadcasts. Some ideas for using the video live stream feature of Instagram include product launches, expert roundups, and exclusive short-term promotional campaigns that only dedicated audiences can capitalize on.

Create A Mini Video Channel

Do you wish to create your own mini video channel on Instagram, without using YouTube or Vimeo as the server platform? If so, you should consider using Instagram's IGTV feature. This was also introduced to Instagram last year, and unlike the video live streaming feature, it has generated a lot of buzz among the brands that are on Instagram, both big and small. IGTV can host videos ranging from ten minutes to an hour, depending on whether your brand profile is verified.

Dos and Don'ts

Here are some important dos and don'ts to keep in mind when putting your social media branding efforts into Instagram:

- Don't try to optimize Instagram posts for SEO. It is extremely difficult to index and rank, and even if you manage to accomplish this extremely difficult task, that SEO effort will vanish with the next Instagram algorithm change. Instead, keep an eye on Instagram insights and modify your posts accordingly to increase your outreach.
- Try to maintain an even flow when sharing

posts on Instagram. If your followers are constantly flooded with your posts on their feed, it will boomerang back on you and possibly lead them to unsubscribe from your Instagram page.

- Buying followers might be a tempting way to gain access to some of the more premium features of Instagram, but don't do it. What will happen is that, like many failed business pages on Facebook, you will end up having a lot of followers with little to no engagement, which will raise red flags to potential real followers who could have been successfully converted into a sales opportunity.

- Avoid posting adult content on your Instagram posts or stories, as this will likely turn off a lot of potential followers and lead to drops in engagement ratios.

- Stick to regular marketing and promotional campaigns, but don't be too pushy. If you come off as trying too hard or create a needy image, your followers will start to doubt your brand and the quality of the products you're offering.

Don't go crazy with your hashtags. Sure, they're your primary means of connecting with audiences and letting your audience engage others with your posts, but excessive use of hashtags often backfires by distracting the audience from your intended core hashtag. This means you should drop irrelevant, trendy hashtags and instead, try using descriptive hashtags that bring out the core theme of the post you intend to share.

Chapter Two: Facebook

Facebook is made for one thing — influencing people to buy your brand, and subsequently, your product. What you sell on Facebook is not your product, but your brand. Your brand is everything that is built around your product — the kind of service, connection to the brand and company name, and the lifestyle you want to portray. People don't buy products anymore simply out of usefulness, they buy products that can add to their sense of being. So, what you need to sell to people is the lifestyle they associate with the product. If buying a product will make them feel like they're part of a trend or, say, helping the environment, they are more likely to engage with your brand. When people look to buy an expensive bag or perfume, what they expect along with it is a luxurious buying experience that makes them feel fancy and cared for.

Of course, not everyone can just open an expensive store and serve champagne to make people feel like, in buying this product, they are buying an entryway into a more prestigious lifestyle. What you can do, though, is create a similar experience through Facebook — which allows you to not only connect with your users on a personal level, but also to study their interests and likes to develop your product experience accordingly. In a way, Facebook is better for selling than regular shops, because of the constant communication and feedback between the customer and the seller. What you need to do to extend the reach of your product is to take this opportunity to study your customer base and create a Facebook Page that not only attracts customers because of the product, but because of brand association.

Brand association and its creation through Facebook is invaluable for your business, because products are replaceable. Perhaps somebody else is selling the same thing, and maybe even at a cheaper rate. The only way to gain a competitive advantage in such a situation is to make people feel more included in your selling process. People buy on the basis of trust, so you must personalize yourself for them.

Showing that you care about the community you are selling in, along with creating relatability by latching on to ongoing trends and culture, is the best way to make people feel that they should exclusively buy your product. It is no secret that Facebook is the most popular social networking website in the world. Over the years, Facebook managed to evolve into an advertising tool for companies, and now plays host to several businesses that use it as a platform to promote their business. Facebook for business is now not just a fad, but a very lucrative concept that more and more companies are identifying with, and incorporating, to avail multiple benefits.

On the face of it, social media marketing is mostly free. However, it takes a sizeable amount of effort to learn how to make the most of this free tool. Of course, that's why this book is so necessary.

Basics Skills for Facebook Marketing

Although most business owners have heard about the powerful effects of social media marketing, few are confident in using it to benefit their businesses. Facebook is not designed to automatically lead you down the path of profitability. No, you need to discover that knowledge yourself. I can help you understand what to post and how to post it in order to move your fans to buy your products. Along the line, you'll learn some key skills that will help your business gain traction in the marketplace. Here are some basics skills that outline everything you need to know about Facebook marketing:

Complete and long-term commitment to Facebook marketing:

The more you understand about how social media marketing works, the easier it will be to commit to using it. And this is a long-term commitment; you don't immediately arrive with a fully-developed Facebook marketing campaign, replete with a page that has a huge, vocal following that draws in and converts customers. It's a continual process involving ongoing self-education. You'll be actively tweaking your marketing approach to stay up-to-date with trends and to take advantage of current events. The Facebook application itself is continually evolving, adding functionality that a savvy marketer can take advantage of to keep one's business on the cutting edge of success.

Understand how social media marketing works:

You'll want to learn how basic marketing principles apply to social media marketing. You'll be discovering how you can implement effective strategies to build a successful Facebook marketing campaign. This goes far beyond just setting up a profile, presenting product images with attractive descriptions, and hoping people find your new site. You'll be discovering some specific strategies used by successful Facebook marketers and learning how to apply them to your business situation.

Turn your fans and followers into loyal customers:

Regardless of how many followers or fans a business has, it doesn't automatically translate into sales. You'll be discovering skills that will help you transform interested individuals into loyal customers.

Understanding the psychology behind buyer behavior:

You'll need to learn what lies behind a customer's decision to buy a product or service. Armed with this knowledge, you can more easily design effective marketing campaigns on Facebook.

Set clear goals for marketing on Facebook:

As you gain a clear image of what can be accomplished through social media marketing, you will be able to establish specific objectives for what you want to see happen and apply practical marketing strategies to get you there.

Learn to capture and convert leads:

Discover what leads look like on Facebook and how you can trap and develop them into paying customers.

Establish reasonable expectations:

Discover what Facebook can and cannot do for you. Learn how to incorporate Facebook marketing activities into your daily routine, as well as your future planning activities.

Learn how to attract the right audience:

With any business, your marketing plan involves knowing your target audience and how to reach it. Once you know these basic principles, you then need to learn how to apply them to the medium of Facebook.

Know how to get a bigger audience:

Most businesses need a sizeable audience to make any type of impact. While engagement is important, that engagement comes from your pool of followers. You'll need to know how to increase the size of this pool to boost the amount of engagement.

Learn to function proactively:

You can't just assume that visitors to your site will press the "like" or "follow" button. Unfortunately, this rarely happens. Learn how to give your visitors a good reason to follow your business.

Learn what to promote:

Social media marketing is not about pushing products; it's about developing trust. Learn how to shift your focus to trust building, and you'll end up selling more products.

Learn how to post effectively:

This can be a little tricky. If you post too frequently, you'll annoy your followers or even be classified as spam. If you post too seldom, you'll not be seen at all. You also need to know what kind of content is most helpful to post and what to stay away from.

The purpose of this section is to help you understand how Facebook works, how Facebook for Business works, and the wonderful things you can do with the platform to reach out to potential buyers and influence them into purchasing your products or services.

Facebook Apps

Facebook is also available on mobile, and can easily be downloaded from the app store. The user interface is extremely friendly and will help you navigate through the different aspects of a typical page. Most people prefer to check the news feed available to them on their homepage and remain updated with the various developments.

Facebook has a number of applications that can be useful for anyone running a social media business portfolio. These applications were made for the sole reason of helping businesses create a strong social media presence.

Facebook Groups is one such application. You can create a Facebook group for your product, business, or just your staff. The main purpose of this application is to manage groups easily; it can be slightly difficult to manage multiple groups. You can review all the posts and interact with the members, and you don't have to open your Facebook app every time for this. Further, you can sort out the notifications for groups because groups tend to spam a lot; this way, you can keep your Facebook id and group-related business separate.

The second app is called Facebook Page Manager — a must for anyone trying to increase the reach of his or her page. Managing a page is not simple and requires a lot of work; it can be hard to deal with page-related issues on the regular app. Page Manager has a brilliant and easy-to-use interface that is perfect for anyone managing a page from their phone. It allows you to customize your page, adjust settings, or address many other issues from your phone, meaning with this app, you can work on the go.

Apps for Business Marketing

There are various apps that every Facebook marketer

must have in order to be more successful. These apps are not officially made by Facebook but are meant to help you in running a business page on the platform by providing help with the content on your page and even with tracking progress.

These apps are fairly straightforward, and they are a must-have for anyone who is running the Facebook page for a business.

Custom Tab Apps

These are the kind of apps that help you to install a small website on your Facebook page. You can have customized videos, images, and other content on a single tab with the help of these apps. Not everybody has brilliant editing and computer skills; if you are one of those people, these apps will do that work for you, allowing you to offer your customers everything that they might need. Recommendations: Hayo and Tabsite.

Email capture apps

These are the apps that will help you capture the email addresses of your Facebook audience without disturbing them. It can be really difficult to get email addresses out of people, and you need these email addresses because it expands your reach. You can get the email address from the people who visit your page by guiding them to click on certain links, so you don't have to ask for email addresses directly. Recommendations: Constant Contact and aWeber.

Quiz and Poll apps

These are the kind of apps that help in preparing polls and surveys to post on your page. Quizzes and polls are an important way to gain customer feedback; the more customer feedback you have, the better you can serve your customers. You need apps for this purpose because it's really difficult to get people interested in taking a short survey or quiz. Quiz and poll apps ensure that whatever you create is viable enough to attract people easily. Recommendations: Woobox and Antavo.

Automatic Posting apps

These are the apps that can be a life-saver for anyone who does not have the time to regularly update the Facebook page of their business. Automatic Posting allows you to create a post now and then schedule when you want that post to publish. The post will appear on your page automatically at the time that you set. This is really helpful because not everyone has the time to regularly post stuff on his or her page, but if you don't post stuff, your page starts to look dead. This gives a very bad impression to any customer who visits. Scheduled posting ensures that your page seems active even when you are too busy to post anything. This can be done directly on Facebook itself, or there are apps that will do it for you. Recommendations: Buffer and Rignite.

Social Media Integration apps

Social media integration is the concept of being able

to use different social media sites with the help of just one app. By using these apps, you can connect different social media sites to your Facebook page, so that whatever you post on other social media sites also appears on your Facebook page. So, if you post something on your Twitter or your Instagram, it will automatically be posted to your Facebook page with the help of Social Media Integration apps. You get a lot of benefit out of this because many users follow a couple of social media sites exclusively, these users might just get connected with you on other social media platforms if they see your Facebook posts. Recommendations: Pagemodo and Tabsite.

Contest apps

Contests apps help you to organize contests on your Facebook page to increase participation in your business and keep your audience interested. Contests can be difficult to organize and take a lot of work; you even have to check the terms and conditions that Facebook has laid out for organizing contests. You can deal with all of this with the help of Contest apps because they make it easier for you to organize a contest, and they make sure that you comply with the terms and conditions of Facebook. Recommendations: Offerpop and Votigo.

Facebook Marketing

Facebook is one of the most innovative markets to use to sell your products. If you correctly tap into the platform's potential, then you will definitely be able to successfully market your products. Facebook Marketing is based on trying to capture the imagination of your audience in new and interesting ways. If you can get your audience to relate to your product, you'll be able to sell it to them.

If you have an established audience, you can definitely use Facebook to influence people so as to create a positive attitude toward your products. A lot of companies are using this strategy; they actually hire Social Media managers — people who are exceptional at handling social media platforms in order to create a positive image for the product and increase its reach. You can do all of this by yourself, however — all you have to do is understand how important Facebook is, set up your page correctly, and understand how advertising works.

Facebook is especially important for small businesses. These businesses do not have a lot of money to invest in expensive advertising campaigns. They can use Facebook to create a fan following for their products and generate enough awareness and revenue to get to that level where you can afford those expensive advertising campaigns.

Connect to Billions of People

Facebook is the biggest social media platform available for any marketer. It has over four hundred million active users, and these are people who actively use their accounts on a daily basis. If you advertise correctly, you can reach out to a lot of these people. You can advertise your product to them and make them aware of who you are and what you offer.

Search Engine Optimization

SEO is important for any business — it's a way to get your business famous on Google. If you have a Facebook page, it will show up first when someone Googles the name of your business. If you do not have a Facebook page, it might be difficult for people to find information about your business. Facebook links are the ones that come up on top whenever you Google something, which is why Facebook pages are really significant.

Competitive Advantage

The best way to get an edge over your competition is with the help of Facebook. It's a really competitive market out there, and everyone is trying to do better than his or her competition. Now, Facebook might just be the edge that you need in order to beat them.

If your competition is on Facebook and you are not, then you are already two steps behind. Facebook can be the difference between you and your competition, which is why Facebook is so important.

There is a lot of competition in the food industry, and almost every restaurant out there has a Facebook page. People even decide where they want to go on the basis of the reviews that they see on the Facebook page of a restaurant. This can be the deciding factor for a customer who is confused between you and your competition, and you have to make sure that you capitalize on this opportunity by having a Facebook presence — and by keeping your page active, as well.

It's Free!

Facebook is simply free promotion. If people like your page, then your content shows up on their news feed. If they comment on your post or share your status, then it further encourages other people to like your page, and they get to know more about your business. This is an absolutely free way of promotion, and you don't have to do anything at all for this. This might not be very effective, and it might take a lot of time to build a huge fan following. Still, even if it helps you to gain a couple of loyal new customers, that's more than enough. You didn't have to spend any money and yet you got a few patrons.

Your page might just go viral, as well. If your posts are interesting and you use interactive stuff like memes, puns, etc. to promote your page, then people will get more interested. They will definitely share stuff like this, and this will earn you an even bigger fan following. Free promotion is really important for any small business, and if you work really hard for it, you will definitely see some benefit.

Direct Interaction through News Feed

People won't see the posts of your page on their news feed just because they have liked your page. Facebook has various ways to determine what posts appear on a person's news feed. More than anything else, the thing that determines someone's news feed is that person's interests. If someone has an interest in a particular thing, all the related posts about that interest will show up on their news feed first.

So, if a person is a huge fan of food and has liked a lot of Facebook pages related to food, they will typically see posts by restaurants they have liked on their news feed.

You can use this to your advantage by posting content that matches those interests. If a person has liked your page, then they obviously have an interest in your business. So, try to post content that is related to your business, but at the same time, is interesting enough to hold a person's attention.

This gives you a great opportunity to get into people's news feeds. You can use this Facebook algorithm to make your page even more famous by posting relevant and interesting content.

Facebook also shows things that are more famous first. The posts that match your interests *and* that your friends have liked are shown first. This is why posting engaging content becomes very important — the more likes and shares you get, the better the chances are of a user seeing your posts in their news feed. You should try out your posts on a specific group of people to see how engaging it is, and this will help in ensuring the long-term viability of your Facebook page.

You have to work on your Facebook analytics; try to see what kind of content gets your audience interested and work on your future content on the basis of these analytics. Always remember who your target audience is so you can customize your content on that basis.

Get Customer Feedback

Customer Feedback is really important because it generates customer loyalty. A customer would always prefer a business that adds a personal touch. The reason for this is pretty simple: every customer wants what is best for him. The business that treats him better and with kindness is the one he would be attracted toward. On Facebook, through posts and comments, you can directly connect with your customers. It's impossible to connect with each person directly in real life. That is why Facebook is so important, as you can reply to each comment and take all of their queries. You can show your customer that you care about them and their needs.

It further creates more customers for you. If a business gives a personal touch to whatever they are doing, then a customer will always prefer that brand. This is because the customer would feel like the business cares about him. A lot of big companies can't connect with each and every one of their customers directly. These customers feel like they are not being heard, and they are not being taken care of. Hence, it's important for them to feel like they matter to your business, and Facebook is the perfect way to do this.

Responding to Problems

You can respond to problems really quickly on Facebook. If there is any issue, you can make a post about it and inform your customers, allowing you to tackle problems in an easy manner. It further helps you respond to the problems of your customers because if a customer has a problem, he can always message you on Facebook. It's difficult for a business to be available at all times, but when you're on Facebook, you are easy to reach. Even if you can't solve the problem at the moment, at least the customer can directly connect with you.

Social Media Presence

Social reputation is not about how many likes you have or how active your user base is. It's simply about having a presence on social media — this is all that you need to have a social reputation. The businesses that are not on Facebook are at an inherent loss, because they will never be able to market their products or services as well as their competitors.

Social reputation is simply about having a page; if you don't have a Facebook page, then you will never have a social reputation. Now, the consequences of not having a social reputation stems from user behavior. A consumer will always prefer those businesses that he believes are legitimate and who work hard to gain customers. You can get this legitimacy by being on Facebook, and many users tend to just search up the name of a business on Facebook to determine if they want to add themselves to your consumer base.

If you are not on Facebook, then there is a sizeable amount of people that may not even take your business seriously, and when they don't take your business seriously, you'll never become a reputed seller for them.

Facebook Page

Facebook bases all its interaction on two things — profiles and pages. A profile basically introduces a person, whereas a page introduces a company or business. A profile is created for an individual looking to represent himself or herself on Facebook, whereas a page is created by an individual to represent his or her company or business. The same individual can create an individual profile for himself, as well as a page for his or her company.

A profile can add friends (others using Facebook and will appear in the list of friends). These can be friends, family members, and acquaintances of the person. The page, on the other hand, can have likes and followers. Likes refer to the number of people who like the particular page, and in turn, the company in question. These can be known or unknown people, as it is impossible to know who has liked a page.

A profile's activity generally shows up in the news feed, as compared to a page's feed. A person has to visit a page in order to know what is happening on the page's feed.

There is also the option to create a group on Facebook. A group basically is a place where like-minded people can collaborate. A person can create a closed or a public group, depending on the creator's preference, and invite others to join in. But it is not possible for a business to own a group and becomes important for one to create a page for it. A business profile can partake in a group, if necessary. We'll talk about groups in detail later on in the book.

The very first step is to create a page. To do this, log onto Facebook.com and click on the 'create a page' button at the bottom. It will be easy if you already have a Facebook account, as you can easily create a page by signing into your existing account. Or, you can enter Facebook.com/pages and create a page. Next, you have to understand the different terms and conditions listed.

Once done, you can enter the name of the page. Remember to take your time — don't rush the decision. It is best to consult with friends and family before coming up with a name for the page. Facebook allows just one change of name once the page has been created.

Then, you can identify the type of business you own. You will have to choose one of the following options.

- Local business or place
- Company, Organization or Institution
- Brand or Product
- Artist, Band or Public Figure
- Entertainment (promotion)
- Cause or Community

Once you choose the appropriate option, you can fill in the 'About' info details before adding your website's address. When you're finished, Facebook will give you your unique URL for your page.

Next, you can choose the preferred page audience, and if you have content for people above 18 years of age, then you have to specify it to your audience. If you are not yet ready with your page, go to the settings and edit the page visibility, choosing "unpublish page" to continue editing the page without being disturbed.

Here are the different page elements you can choose:

Settings

Page visibility — Here, you can choose who can view your page. If you are keen on making it a private page, then you can modify the settings and make it a closed group.

Posting visibility — Here, you can choose who can post on your page. Sometimes, it's important to limit the posts so you don't end up with a page consisting of a million posts.

Targeting and privacy for posts — This is to capture a particular audience. It is important to gear the posts to a certain audience, so you send the message across to the right people.

Messages — The messages that your page can receive. If you are taking orders from people through your Facebook profile, then you can create filters to keep the spam at bay.

Tagging ability — People who can tag your page.

Country restrictions — People from specific countries that can view your page. Sometimes it's best to limit the page to only those countries where your business operates, so you don't receive spam.

Age restrictions — People of specific age groups can view your page.

Page moderation — This allows you to prevent certain words from appearing on your page, thereby staving off spamming.

Profanity filter — This is to prevent people from using profane words.

Comment Ranking — This highlights the comments with the highest number of likes or comments.

Delete a page — You can delete a page if you don't like it and start from scratch.

Category — Pick a category for your company; this is quite important as people will find it easy to look for you.

Name — The name of your company.

Start information — The details of when your company started.

Short description — A short description of your company.

Long description — A detailed description of what your company is all about.

Company overview — A brief overview of your company such as the location, history, legal structure, management, etc.

Mission — Your company's goal and your overall approach to realize those goals.

When founded — The date when your company was founded.

Awards — Any awards have come your company's way.

Phone number — Your company's phone number.

Website — Your company's website.

Once you fill in the above details, your page will be

ready to roll!

Here is a look at the Facebook page standards:

Profile Picture

The specifications for your profile picture are:

- The picture must be square.
- It must be at least 180x180 pixels.
- It should display at 160x160 pixels on a computer.
- It should display at 140x140 pixels on smartphones.
- It should be 50x50 pixels on feature phones.
- You must leave a space around, so the picture does not go all the way to the edge.
- It is best for companies and businesses to use the company logo.

Cover photo

For the cover picture:

- It is recommended to use an 851x315 pixels,

RGB, JPG picture that is less than 100 kb.

- You can use the graph provided by Facebook to crop the image to the right size. It is best to use a picture that is easy on the eyes and not too overwhelming.

Calls to Actions

- Remember that it is extremely important for you to guide your audience and tell them what to do on your page. Many people assume that people by themselves understand whatever they are supposed to do on a page; however, it pays to give them a clear instruction.

- It is best to create a "call to action" button that will allow your audience to take appropriate action. You must also expressly mention it in words to drive home the message.

Facebook Posts

Here are the specifications for Facebook posts:

- The news feed images should be 472x394 pixels and have an actual ratio of 236x197 pixels, and the image should be 504x504.

If you need help with this specification then here are some tools that you can use to edit the picture, including Picmonkey.com and Canva.com.

Posting to page

- You can post unique links to your page by adding them to the page.
- You can choose a picture and post it on the page.
- You can schedule your posts to publish at regular intervals.
- You can edit the picture by hitting the edit button, and you will have a glimpse of how others are seeing it.
- If you do edit it, you can copy the new link and paste it in the box.
- It is best to check all your work before posting it to avoid having to delete it later.
- It is convenient to post multiple pictures at once.
- You can add a short description to each post.
- You can easily tag people in your pictures.
- You can use the # to look for someone who has been tagged.
- You can also tag posts the same way and look

for them using the #.

Additional things to do on Pages

- When you upload a picture or a video, you have the option of adding your location. But it will pay to exercise a little precaution and post location only if necessary.
- The video you wish to upload should be of a certain size. You can check the limitation of the video before uploading it.
- You will be notified once your photos and videos have been uploaded.
- Remember, videos will not automatically upload the audio, and you must add it separately.
- For the event milestones tab, you can check the drop-down options and choose the options that suit your requirements.
- You can use the milestones option to read about the company, its various posts and the different people who can post on it.
- You can control the various tabs by clicking the "manage tabs" option and edit them to your liking.
- One important point to note while posting on

a company page is to log out as the admin and log into your personal profile before making a comment. If you have hired someone to manage the page, they can be instructed to reply through the account or create another one.

- Remember, it is extremely important to share your business page on your personal timeline as it helps with capturing a bigger audience. After all, the main motivation behind creating a page is to gather as big a crowd as possible, so it is important to advertise it extensively to be noticed by as many people as possible.

- Remember that your page is synonymous with your company, and vice versa. You have to maintain a professional tone while posting on the page and instruct any other employees to do the same.

Strategies for Your Posts

Facebook is fundamentally based on posts and their ability to go 'viral' – which means that your content has to be so encapsulating that it draws people in. Here are some strategies for viral Facebook posts:

Use Emotions

Facebook is not really about selling products – it's about actually connecting with people. You can't connect with people unless you are selling emotions. It doesn't really matter what your product is — on Facebook, if you want people to care about your page and your brand, you have to connect with them emotionally.

The only way you can connect with people is by associating the utility of your product with things that make people relate to it. So, if you're trying to sell, say clothes, you can't just show people what you offer and hope that they wear it. If you instead put up a story of how your clothes are made and showcase the people who work endlessly to ensure that the clothes you make are perfect, you're far more likely to gain public attention.

Don't Overdo It

Of course, trying to connect with your potential audience is important, but make sure that you're not trying too hard. If you latch on to every new trend and joke around too much, it's eventually going to saturate your audience. Also, many brands think they can connect to the younger generation by using their slang and style, but try not to partake in silly things like this. It's only going to make your posts seem fake, and as though you're trying to be relatable just for the sake of it.

It's important to remember that you're selling something, at the end of the day. If you're going to try your hardest to make it seem otherwise, it's only going to make your audience unreactive to what you have to say.

Keep Posts Short & Specific

The one key element of Facebook marketing is to keep your customer's attention – if your customer sees posts that are too long, or if your all your posts are videos, they're not going to engage a lot.

Be direct with your audience and tell them what you're selling, while trying to connect with them at the same time. Most brands tend to have far more success with shorter posts than they do with huge advertising campaigns.

If you do decide to make longer posts, remember to add pictures and paragraphs. This will at least make your audience interested enough to continue reading.

Facebook Strategies

When it comes to setting up a killer page on Facebook, it is important to make it as interesting for your audience as you can. You must put in the effort to make it look as professional as possible, as well, to help your audience connect with it more effectively.

Here are some strategies that you can employ to make your Facebook page entertaining for your audience:

Personality

It is important for you to add a certain amount of personality to your Facebook page. People should be drawn in by it and feel the urge to like or comment on your content. If you settle for something mediocre, then it will not work in your favor. A good idea is to hire professionals who are good at molding pages and making them interesting for the audience. Instruct them to review your target audience and prepare an analysis of their general characteristics. Doing so helps in preparing a fitting schedule that will make your page popular. You can also look at the strategies that other companies are employing and come up with a plan that is in keeping with the same. However, it is best to maintain a little originality and remain true to your company's policies.

It pays to have a good sense of who you are and what your company stands for. If you remain confused, this will work against you. It is best to develop an image that you would like to portray and then pursue the same. Remember that things can look like one thing in your mind and another on paper. So it is best to create a page and ensure it looks exactly like you planned it.

Consistency

Remember that consistency is key. You have to be consistent with your posts, and they should be coherent. Your Facebook page should be a slice of your store and the products you sell there. Don't make it too different, as this can confuse your customers. If you have a team working for you, instruct them to post content at regular intervals and not keep the audience waiting. A good trick is to know when people prefer to see an update come their way and schedule your content to publish during those times. But don't make it boring, as you want to keep your audience engaged. Again, you can look at a successful company's strategy and come up with a posting schedule that suits your own business. As mentioned earlier, it is best to aim for the early evening slot, as that's when most people are active online.

Frequency

When it comes to maintaining an online profile for your company, it is extremely important to update often. You must try to schedule new posts at regular intervals so people know what to expect and when to expect them. A golden rule is to post in the evenings, as that is when most people expect new content. Try to increase the frequency of the posts as and when the company grows. Some companies prefer to post new posts thrice a day, as that helps in keeping the audience glued. But it is important not to get carried away and post too many things all at once. You cannot overload the audience with too much information, as it will end up confusing them. Keep the information relevant and coherent. You can always do a short trial and error to see what is working for you and what isn't. For example, you can ask your audience how often they would like to receive an email from you. If they are happy with the frequency, you can maintain it, or change it according to their preferences.

Business Goals

It is quite important to be in sync with your business goals and update your page from time to time by keeping in mind your main motivations. Your page should be a thorough representation of your company speaking to your ambitions and portraying your true intentions. It pays to incorporate a little of your company's policies in every new post.

Converting your Profile to a Business Page

If you already have a Facebook profile and wish to convert it into a page without creating a separate one, you can do so easily. Here are some simple instructions:

At the top right-hand corner of your Facebook profile, you will find a drop-down button. Under that, you will find "manage pages", which gives you the option to "create a page." Click here, and you will be able to add a page to your current profile. There, you will be able to automatically convert your current profile into a page.

You can also merge your profile with your page. Click settings and download a copy of your Facebook page, then select the profile to page migration option. Remember, once it is merged, you won't be able to retrieve your profile. You have to make up your mind before making the transition. To merge your business page, go to settings, choose the general tab, and select either the merge pages and merge duplicate pages, then choose the pages that you want to merge. But remember, the two pages have to be identical — including same exact address and information — otherwise, they will not merge into one.

It is easier to create a brand-new page dedicated to your company. However, you will have to fill in all the different details from scratch.

Merchandize

It is a good idea to start with the merchandise. This

includes offering exclusive goods that are not available at the store. For example, you can offer a new product that people can only buy through your Facebook page or website and not at the store. Alternately, you can offer a customized product that is exclusively available online. Say, for example, you offer to customize a product to the customer's liking by changing the color scheme or encrypting a message, etc. You can also offer a product in a color scheme or pattern that is different from whatever is available in the store. Make it obvious by posting appropriate announcements and tell your customers they are online exclusives. You can also tell the people in your store to check it out online in order to direct their attention to your Facebook page.

Offers

You can run exclusive online offers, as well. These can include schemes such as buy one get one free, or get a complimentary gift, etc. Such offers are sure to generate interest and enhance your page's value. Again, it is important to advertise, so people are made aware of the offer. You can send out emails detailing the same and tell people about the offers you have made available to your online audience. You can also advertise it in your store or hand out flyers to people, encouraging them to visit your Facebook page.

Rewards

You can reward people who bring in a specific number of likes, too. This works well as people will be prompted to bring in more and more potential new customers to like your page. The reward needs to be a little appealing in order to capture your audience's interest. You can offer coupons, free merchandise, or specially-designed merchandise. All of these will prove to be quite appealing and help lure in more people to like your page. You can make an announcement on the page as well as on your other social media accounts. You can also mention it on your website and inform the people who visit your physical store.

Discount coupons

You can offer discount coupons and discounts to your customers. These coupons will allow them to pay a lower amount for the products and services that you have on offer in your store. They will be able to avail these coupons only on the Facebook page. Again, you must announce it on all your social media accounts, such as Twitter and Instagram, to inform people.

Contests

Contests are a fun way to get people to visit your

page. These help people get involved in an exciting way. The contest should be related to the products or services that you offer, like adding a tagline or completing a phrase or posting pictures of the products. You can announce the contest on your Facebook page, and ensure that you also announce a good prize that will excite people enough to partake in the contest. Setting a short deadline is a must, as you will have the chance to increase your page views in a short period of time.

Events

You can also announce events, where people can meet up and get to know each other better. Such events will also help you know your own audience. You can organize food and drinks, as well.

Events can help you out a lot if they are done correctly. All you have to do is create an interesting event, invite as many people as you can, and spread awareness with the help of your page. The benefit from this is that you don't have to spend a ton of money sponsoring events organized by other people — a lot of people sponsor local events to get name recognition.

However, you can use Facebook to gain name recognition without spending a lot of money through events. Events can become very well-known if they are publicized in the right way. First, you'll need to identify the kind of event that your target audience would be interested in. Once you have done that, start inviting people and spread the word about the event.

Say you are a local bakery who wants name recognition in your locality. Start by thinking of a creative event you can use to publicize your business while also giving your customers a fun time. Create a related event on Facebook and start inviting people that you know are in your area; use your contacts as well as your Facebook page. Use the event to promote your company, and keep publicizing your bakery so that your small business gets name recognition.

This is just the start — by spending a little more money, you can create events that will attract thousands of people. Start slowly with events that won't require a significant investment, and once you see that the events are helping streamline revenue, you can start expanding to bigger events to get even more name recognition.

These are just some of the different offers you can run online, and are not limited to just these. You can modify them all to suit your company's policies.

Facebook Ads

In the previous section, we looked at Facebook pages in detail. In this one, we look at Facebook ads. Ads are what companies use to advertise their products or services on Facebook. As mentioned earlier, it is quite important for companies to put out information about their products, so more people are made aware of them.

These Facebook ads are mostly displayed on the right corner of the platform, but you can choose where to place them on the page. You can do so by changing the settings.

You can read on the subject by accessing the "Facebook ads guide." You will have the chance to educate yourself about the types of ads that can be created. Here are some of the choices you will find:

- Click to a website — This will take you directly to the destined site.

- Review design recommendations — You can review the designs that can be incorporated in the ads.

- Carousel — The carousel will help your audience view multiple products and services at once.

You can add in tracking to see how many leads you have captured, and make sure you leave behind a "call-to-action" option that your audience can click on to take appropriate action.

There is a big difference between the ads that play on the website and the ones on the app. You have to customize the ads to fit well with the app. Here are the steps you should take for the same:

- You must first install the app and have a clear idea of how ads will look like on it.
- Next, you must see how engaged your audience will be.
- You need to be aware of local events and happenings in order to appeal to your audience.
- You should keep track of other company's offers and try to compete with these as much as possible.
- Remember, it is important to distinguish between your website views and mobile views.

You can make use of a video testing tool to check the ads before they go live.

Facebook advertising is a very powerful tool you can use to promote your products and services. Advertising on Facebook is very easy once you know how to go about the process.

Getting started is simple. Once you have your ad permit, go to the "manage your ads" button on

Facebook.com/adsmanage and choose the options you would like to incorporate in your advertising feature.

If you wish to create an ad from scratch, here are the steps to follow:

- Choose the type of ad you wish to control. This depends on what you want the ad to stand for.

- Next, choose the objective of your campaign and incorporate it into the ad as extensively as possible.

- Next, choose the demographic for whom the ad will be displayed. Doing so will help your ad connect better with the chosen audience.

- Next, decide on the budget you wish to allot for the ad. It pays to have a number in mind, as this helps you stay on track and prevents overspending. You can set the budget based on how big you want the ad to be.

- Next, you must create an audience for your ads. You should keep in mind the audience that will be viewing your ads and incorporate elements that will please them.

Creating a Page-Like Ad

When it comes to creating a Facebook ad, you have to follow a few steps that will make your ad accessible to your audience.

- You can start by creating the ad, which will be explained in detail under the 'Creating Ads' in a later section in this chapter.

- Remember that it is important to promote your Facebook page so more and more people have the chance to view your ads.

- It's important to set a budget for your video ads. If you don't, you run the risk of overspending.

- It is important to pick the right demographics to show the ads in order to make a big impact. If you create an ad that does not appeal to the chosen demographic, it will end up being a wasteful campaign.

- It is important to choose the right campaign name for your ad, as this will greatly help capture your audience's attention

- You must make use of thoughtful pictures that speak to your chosen audience.

Creating Audiences

It is no secret that your ads will not work if you don't create an appropriate audience for them. Here is how you can achieve this:

- Click on the Audience tab to choose the right audience for your work.

- Customize the audience that you already know and pick out people who suit your campaign the best.

- You can choose where your audience comes from. For example, it can be from your friend list or from your Facebook Page.

- You can upload a list of people, import them, or pick out specific people from your list contacts.

- Next, you should agree to the terms that Facebook puts forth.

- It is best to name your audience so you know what they comprise — for example, if it is a group of teenagers, you can name it "teens." This way, you can save a target group and name it to create specific ads for them.

- It is a good idea to test your ad with a dummy audience to see if it clicks with them.

- Once you create the ad, you can import your audience over.

- You can upload appropriate images to suit your ad campaign.

- You can choose how long the ad will run on Facebook.

- Remember, all the ads go through a screening process, so it is best to preview the ad before going live with it.

- It is extremely important to create an audience for all your ads.

- The target groups will be chosen based on demographics.

- You can avail a graph that will show you the size of the demographics.

Creating Ads

- Click on the create ads tab.

- Choose the objective of the ad.

- Add in the name of the campaign in order to facilitate future reference.

- You can either choose an audience or create one from scratch. You can also import an audience from your page.

- It is vital to add demographics in order to capture the right audience.

- You can pick the options to add in multiple images or a single image.

- You can always connect to your personal Facebook profile.

- You can click on the languages tab to pick the language of choice.

- It is extremely important to add in a call to action to help people take the desired course of action.

- You can generate a conversion tracker to keep a tab of your conversions.

- You must create a pixel, which is a code that collects data of your conversions.

- You should keep track of the page views.

- Make a note of the URL.

- You have to validate the ad that you create.

- You can edit your ad by clicking on the "campaigns" tab.

- You can use an old ad to serve as a base for another ad by changing up the images, keeping the basic concept of the ad intact.

Video Ads

Video ads are much better than picture ads as they will capture your audience's attention in a more dramatic way. Here are the steps that you can adopt to create video ads:

- Start by creating a plan for the ad.

- Next, choose your target audience — just as you would for your regular ads, you will have to choose the right demographics for your video ads.

- Next, plan the budget for the ad. As with regular ads, it is best to set aside a budget, as it will help you stay on course.

- You should upload a video that has the specifications of 720p, and a ratio of 16x9.

- You must preview the ad before it goes live so you can make any necessary changes.

Reports

It is important to look at reports in order to understand how your ads are faring. Start by clicking on the "reports" tab present on the left side of your Facebook page.

There, you will find the following options:

- General metrics
- Choose demographics to look at
- Export as excel file

The cost per click option will show you how much you are making through the clicks on your ads, and you can easily filter the results to see what is working well for you and what is not.

If you have hired a team to look into the analytics, you can add people you want to have access to the account and make desired changes. You can set up an email notification if you want to be notified for the clicks, or you can always access your account history to peek into any activity.

Remember that it is important for you to treat your Facebook page as a primary tool to communicate with your audience and update them about the company's latest developments. Don't get carried away and post things that are of a personal nature. It is also best to not argue with any of the customers posting on the page. You can hire a team to answer customer queries and try to post new content as frequently as possible.

Be enthusiastic and do not allow the page to go cold.

Facebook Groups

In this section, we will look at how you can use three important features of Facebook — groups, analytics, and live — to help your business succeed.

Groups are small communities on Facebook, and you can join over 6,000 of them. If you want to join a group, just click on the Groups tab on your Facebook profile and you'll be redirected to the Discover Groups page. On this page, you can search for different groups by using keywords or find groups based on pages you've liked or the interests Facebook is aware you have.

For a business, the best thing to do is just to search for the kind of business that you do. If you sell clothes, type "clothes," and you'll find multiple groups where people are discussion or recommending clothes.

Some groups are public, while others are private. If it's a closed group, you will have to send a join request which will have to be approved by an admin. You can click on the description of a group to find out the rules of engaging in that group. It's better to follow these rules; otherwise, you might get kicked out.

Groups are great for marketing, especially from a business point of view, because they allow you to interact with a highly-targeted audience. People join groups only if they have a specific need, and they expect people in that group to fulfill that need. With groups, you can increase your awareness about what your customers want while also directly advertising your business to them.

Creating your Own Group

For a business, the best thing you can do is create a community around your product. This way, you'll be able to talk directly to your customers and make sure these customers are engaging with what you're saying. Unlike pages, groups are far more interactive, and you will have active customers who will care about what you're selling.

You can create a group by clicking on the Groups tab on the left-hand side of your profile. You'll have to give your group a name, first – and make sure that this name is catchy. After that, add a few friends of yours to get started.

Set your group up by adding a cover photo that will entice customers. Now, what you need is an audience.

If you want to get more people to join your group, there are a few things you can do. Try promoting your group on your website and Facebook page, and if this doesn't work, get access to email subscription lists for the field of business you're in and mail the group invite to potential customers.

Facebook Analytics

Facebook is a platform that has a diverse amount of users — each with a different way of interacting with your page and your brand. Facebook Analytics helps you market your products effectively by giving you detailed information about potential customers who follow your page. With this information, you can create targeted posts and learn about the kind of interaction that is popular with your audience.

To start, go to your Facebook business page and click on Insight. The three sections that will appear tell you three important things about your page – the number of people who have liked your page in the last week, people who saw your posts and people who engaged with your content. Engagement means liking, sharing, or commenting on what you've posted.

Learning more about the page likes is great for your business, because it not only tells you about how many followers you're gaining, but also explains where you're getting likes. So, you'll see if people like your page because of your posts or because of a Facebook ad. If you want to specifically find out the contribution of a particular ad campaign on the number of likes you received, you can focus on a specific time period.

The next section is the post reach section, and it's the most important one. This will show you how many people saw your posts and how many of them actually interacted with it by liking, sharing, or commenting. This way, you can find out what kinds of posts create more engagement with your audience, identify the posts that lead to more interactions, and continue creating those types of posts.

Strategies for Facebook in 2019

- The stories feature that has been integrated into Facebook has resulted in interesting changes in how audiences are now interacting with content. The takeaway here is to entice the audience to engage with your social media posts and content by giving them a brief glimpse of it through the story feature. If it catches their fancy, they will likely visit your Facebook business page to see the full content. They will also try to learn what your brand is all about if they are only given a vague idea about it.

- Creating viral posts is still a viable technique for sudden and extreme brand exposure. Combine this with the new stories feature, and you have potential brand-building dynamite at your fingertips.

- Video content trumps other forms of social media content in 2019. However, there are some rules to be followed here. Unlike website visitors, who actively search for your brand through search engines to see in-depth videos and other content, social media users are not actively looking for it. This means the videos you make for social media platforms need to be short in length (no more than 60 seconds as a rule of thumb) since Facebook users are constantly scrolling down and don't like their feed to be interrupted by anything lengthy.

- Image-based content comes second to video content on Facebook, which is good news since this means that one of the most major and viable social media posting tactics over the last couple of years still hasn't changed much. Images are still powerful tools, especially if you don't have the budget or skills to make frequent video posts. In certain cases, images can even convey a brand message more clearly than a 30-second video clip.

- Use a post length of 50-150 characters. Instead of long captions and wordy posts akin to usual sales copy, social media sales copy should be shorter and catchier. Remember that you will be competing with an increasing number of new brands every single day who are all vying for attention from the same audience as you are. This has significantly decreased the audience's attention span. Whereas Facebook users were more likely to go through a lengthy advertisement post back in 2013, the same no longer applies today.

- Make your Facebook posts inspirational, engaging, and funny. Tell a story — a good story engages audiences better than anything else. Why else are some of the best Facebook video posts and images narrative-based? Find a story for your brand, structure the narrative, and build your social media posts around it. Make the story enticing so the audience feels compelled to learn more by clicking the link to your website that you will include with the post.

- Learn to build intrigue for your brand through Facebook posts by creating unique Facebook marketing campaigns. This is one of the best social media marketing strategies that has been successfully demonstrated throughout the first quarter of this year by Lionsgate Films for their epic action franchise, John Wick Parabellum. In February, they began posting cryptic posts and statuses that piqued the interest of fans and non-fans alike, who have been constantly bombarded with hype-building posts for movies like Marvel's Avengers Endgame — where the hype was amped up by showing clips, images, and teasers of the film on social media. Lionsgate went a step further and launched a Facebook marketing campaign that allowed certain segments of their audience to receive posts about the movie and cast them an hour earlier than others through a smart subscription campaign. This led to a lot of speculation and word-of-mouth hype. Subscribed users received texts in a similar fashion to how texts are sent out to the assassins in the movie, making them feel like part of the John Wick brand. Creating intrigue and letting your audience's imaginations run wild will greatly benefit your brand if the products and services you are offering are unique and valuable.

One of the easiest ways to develop your personal brand on social media is by establishing yourself as an authority on a particular subject or niche. Digital marketers do this all the time — the trick here is combining a narrative and an offer at the same time. Tell stories of your personal success, and offer your success strategies for free through your own website. You need to have a really strong content game to succeed this way.

Create an offer post that will lead the audience to your website, from where they can download the free resources offered by you in exchange for providing a few personal details; you will be collecting these details to provide them with even more information via email newsletters and updates. This will keep your audience engaged with your brand by providing them with a content loop.

Your newsletters and updates can contain links to further social media posts, which will re-engage the audience on your social media page through emails. Don't be afraid to share your knowledge — the more your followers and audience are likely to believe that you have additional tricks up your sleeve, the more likely it is that they will engage with your brand to find more value.

Chapter Three: LinkedIn

LinkedIn is a very powerful platform for anyone who wants to boost their professional status and make connections with like-minded, ambitious individuals. It offers you many advantages, as a professional, so it becomes paramount to be aware of the potential of this platform and know how to use it to your benefit.

Everyone uses LinkedIn these days, from individuals to businesses to non-profit organizations. Everyone understands the power of a brand, and they all want to reap its benefits by making a name for themselves. LinkedIn is an amazing tool to help in this area.

Here's the thing about any social media profile you use professionally – if you're not visible to the people you're targeting, it doesn't matter how great your profile looks. People should be able to easily find you easily. Moreover, people should see you when they search for people of your trade, be it on LinkedIn or on a regular search engine. For that, you have to make it a priority to tweak your profile in such a way that it becomes more visible.

Your LinkedIn profile can be seen by anyone, regardless of whether they are a LinkedIn user or not. This is because your profile has two components. One is visible only to LinkedIn users, and the other is visible to everyone who searches for you on the

Internet.

To improve the visibility of your profile, you'll need to look at both components. Our goal is to create such an excellent public component that people can't resist checking your full profile. Keeping that in mind, let's take a look at some tips you can use to increase your profile's visibility.

Do's and Don'ts

Do's

In this section, we'll take a look at some simple actions that you can employ quickly. These will take you very little time, say, around 8-10 minutes each. You can even do them when you take breaks from work.

Use a recent, professional photo

Your photo is a window into your personality as it can tell anyone visiting your profile a lot about you. In our world, appearances play a huge role, so you'd be wise not to underestimate the value a good, professionally shot photograph has in attracting people to your profile. Countless studies have been conducted in this regard, and the general conclusion seems to be that professional-looking photos of your head and shoulders are the best.

Discard that cropped party-time photo (or worse, a selfie) you're currently using your profile photo and put up one taken by a professional. It will inspire confidence and trust in people who see your profile.

Use a good headline

When people visit your profile, one of the first things they will notice is your headline —it goes without saying that this is therefore one of the most important parts of your profile. If you've been using LinkedIn for a few years, you might have noticed that every time you change your job, LinkedIn defaults to the job title as your profile headline. This, admittedly, is not the greatest way to appeal to recruiters. You need something personal, unique, and compelling. Think about a new, powerful headline for your profile each time you switch jobs or get promoted. This keeps your profile fresh and appealing.

Follow the right people

To stay in the know and ahead of average Joes, you need to be aware of what the top personalities in your industry are up to. The industry leaders are the people who influence the world and bring change. And this goes beyond — they inspire success in others! Make sure you're following the right people on LinkedIn to get valuable advice and relevant news on a daily basis. Regardless of your industry or experience level, you have to start somewhere — don't worry too much about it. Just start with a few key personalities, and build up from there.

Keep your current responsibilities updated

This one is especially important for those who have recently changed jobs or have been promoted. When that happens, you might be so busy getting used to your new role and responsibilities that social networking can take a back seat. But with a new job comes the need to update your profile, to ensure it accurately reflects your current job profile. Nobody wants to contact a person on LinkedIn to fill a particular role only to later find out that the person contacted is not actually handling the necessary responsibilities at their current job.

Keep your current position, job title, location, and responsibilities up to date and, whenever possible, add some media content to your profile to show your work off to potential recruiters. This works as a portfolio and also makes your profile look aesthetically more pleasing. Double score!

Curate your groups

LinkedIn suggests groups that may be relevant to you and your industry when you first register as a user. Most people initially skip this part, but a few might decide to join every single option suggested by the site. That's okay — a new user doesn't know any better. But most of us don't go back to a group after joining it.

However, groups are actually really important to be

a part of the community and make more meaningful connections. So log in to your LinkedIn account at least once a day and go through new posts in your favorite groups. Also, take a few moments to reevaluate all your groups so you know which ones are irrelevant or useless now and can be deleted. You don't have to join all groups related to your industry, because that can be excessively time-consuming, but pick two or three groups that you find interesting and keep up with those.

Also, join your university's alumni group, if possible. Staying connected to your roots is very beneficial, as you'll always know what's going on at your university and what kind of people are coming out. You can network with freshers and find new talent for your own ventures. And you can even find some career advancement opportunities in these groups. Stay on the lookout!

Ask for a recommendation

After clearing a couple of rounds of interviews, you'll make it to a stage where your prospective employers are bound to ask for some references. In those situations, LinkedIn recommendations work like a charm. They're perfect, because they're by people who already think highly of you and have endorsed you for the skills you've taken the interviews for. They are social proof of things you are good at.

This is why LinkedIn recommendations are so important. They increase your reputation when they come from reputable people with a good work ethic. Make sure you reach out on LinkedIn to people you've worked closely with in the past or currently work with. They can be your coworkers, supervisors, or even clients. Ensure your request is personal and polite. You can mention why a particular person is perfect for writing a recommendation for you, which will make them feel special and increase your chances of getting a good recommendation. And don't forget to write them a recommendation in return.

Filter your endorsements

People on LinkedIn endorse each other's skills quite often, so chances are, you'll also see endorsement for your skills if you have a decent-sized network. As a beginner, we often add everything we're endorsed for on our profile, which can lead to skewed metrics when people visit our profiles and see our endorsed skills. This is why you need to filter out any endorsements that shouldn't be there, at least not high up on the list. Some skills look great at the top because they are relevant to your industry. Others, like Microsoft PowerPoint and the likes, don't look so great. Take the time to filter out such endorsements.

Connect with your team

This is hands-down the easiest thing to follow in all the tips mentioned in this chapter. All you need to do is look up your colleagues on LinkedIn and then connect with them. If your team is fairly large, like a whole department, that's great. If it is very small, you could look at connecting with people beyond your team, too. Just make sure you know these people on some level. If you do connect with people you don't know well, you could use this as an opportunity, too — you just need to embrace it and not be awkward about it. This is a chance for you to say hi and get to know the person by asking them out for a coffee or tea.

Don'ts

For everything you do right to improve your profile, there are twice the number of things you can do wrong. In this chapter, I'll list some pretty common things you should avoid doing if you want a stellar profile.

No spam messages

One really important thing you need to understand before you make a pitch to a potential client, investor, or someone else is that people hate self-serving messages. They will detect it in the first couple of lines and won't bother to read more. Keep this in mind, and don't send spam messages to people on LinkedIn. Take the time to write messages that are well thought-out and customized for different people. Your messages should be beneficial to them. If they're not, you won't have any luck.

Only legitimate recommendations

This is very important to be mindful of. You must never ask people you don't know well for recommendations, and neither should you give them recommendations. This doesn't bode well for your profile. Recommendations are a way of saying you vouch for the person, so if you cannot personally vouch for someone, don't give them or ask them for a recommendation. If their reputation is poor, it will look bad on you.

No negativity in groups

LinkedIn groups are supposed to be helpful and supportive, with lots of meaningful discussions. Don't be the person who brings negativity into the group by being scathing and unnecessarily critical of everything. Sure, there will always be disagreements, but they don't need to be hostile. Make sure your criticism is valid, constructive, and called for.

Don't post too much

LinkedIn has a very professional environment — understandably, since it's a professional network. This is not Facebook. You shouldn't post a status update every time you have something new on your mind. Limit your status updates on LinkedIn to one per day, two at max.

No self-serving content in groups

Like I said above, groups are supposed to be positive and helpful. If you're posting self-serving, spammy content, this helps nobody. Imagine everyone in the groups you are a part of doing the same — there would be no meaningful discussion in any group, ever. That is in nobody's interest. So to avoid this, craft your content for the particular forum you're posting in, and make sure it is of value to the target audience.

Don't promote your Facebook page

There's a certain LinkedIn etiquette you should be aware of when using the website. It asks you to be mindful of your conduct and behave professionally at all times. One of the most common mistakes new people make on LinkedIn is to beg for "likes" on their Facebook pages. I cannot begin to describe how unattractive this is, and how much it hurts your reputation. If you do this, you will be seen as desperate and good-for-nothing. Only mention your Facebook page to another user when you've built a good professional relationship with them. That means messages like "Please like my page" are out of the question.

Be careful of this setting

"Allow recipients to see each other's names and email addresses."

This is an option when sending messages to multiple people at once. Always make sure that this is toggled off when you're sending such messages, unless it's to people you already know well and they don't care whether the message is personalized for them or not. People you don't know well won't like getting random messages that are meant for ten other people. They like personalized messages that make them feel special.

"I see you viewed my profile…" is a big NO

Yes, you heard me. It's creepy as hell and doesn't make the other person want to connect with you. In fact, if anything, it only hurts your chances. Don't start your messages to people by saying this — if you want to connect with someone, write a personalized message in the connection request. Do not include this phrase!

LinkedIn is different from other social networks

People often tend to forget this or are not aware of this at all, and this hurts their reputation on the platform. Like I mentioned before, being on LinkedIn means you need to follow some etiquette, similar to Reddit. The first thing you need to remember is that this is not Twitter or Facebook. It's a completely different type of network that has specific purposes, and one should not use it outside of those purposes. For example, don't post status updates about what you had for lunch on LinkedIn.

Don't ask new connections to endorse you

You may see random people endorsing you for particular skills and realize you hardly know this person at all. This could make you think that asking strangers and new connections for endorsements is okay, but let me tell you, it isn't. Endorse only the people you know well — and the same goes for asking for endorsements.

Do away with standard invitations

Saying "I'd like to add you to my professional network" is the quickest way to tell someone they're not worth a few seconds of your time. It's boring, it's unappealing, and it turns them off. Stop using the standard invitation text and write a personal message, instead. Yes, it seems like a lot of work, but it's worth the effort. Make sure you know whether or not the other person is already on LinkedIn. If not, offer to help them out with it. Keep the message short and to the point. You can use the same custom messages for a few people with the same expertise, but not too many of them.

Keep your expectations flexible

People are different, and they all network differently — don't have rigid expectations when it comes to LinkedIn networking. It can cause unnecessary frustration and discourage you from building healthy relationships with talented people. Be mindful of the following things:

1. Don't judge people for how they network. People do what they feel is right for them; hence, they have different standards when it comes to networking. Also, remember that some people network for reasons above and beyond just networking.

2. Don't expect a quick response all the time. People have lives, and they are busy. Not everyone will respond in a timely manner. And, with this, you should also remember that not everyone is interested in the kind of professional relationship you want. You can try from your end, but don't expect a reciprocal response from the other person.

3. Don't assume things when you see someone's contact list is private. They may have good reasons to do so — and they have every right to do so, too. Keeping things private is not a professional sin.

4. If you're not sure whether someone will recognize you, don't send them a connection request pronto. Try sending them an email or an SMS first to let them know you want to connect with them professionally. Hey, some people are just bad with names!

Don't go in unprepared

Most people who have a decent reputation in any industry will have proper information available on their profile with regards to how you should contact them. It can be both implied and direct, and you need to be aware of this before you initiate dialog with them. You have a responsibility to contact people in their preferred mode of communication and not come off as a nuisance.

Pay attention to people's profiles, review their

contact settings, and respect their privacy and what they're trying to convey with their profile. Listen more and speak less, figuratively speaking. This shows that you did your homework and took the time to prepare. People will appreciate you for it.

Don't disregard LinkedIn messages

LinkedIn messages are not any less important than your Facebook messages and your emails, so don't treat them like a second-class option. Many people think that LinkedIn messages are not time-sensitive, or that they're not as official as a phone call or an email. They're wrong. Make sure email notifications for your LinkedIn messages are always turned on, and check your inbox daily. Also, respond to your messages yourself, instead of delegating it or ignoring the task altogether.

Quantity is not quality

As with most other things in life, quantity and quality are two very different things — and one may not imply the other, in most cases. Doing something a lot doesn't mean it's being done well. If you really want to know how well you're doing something on LinkedIn and would like to track your progress with actual numbers, there are certain business metrics available on the website to help you out, including leads generated, interviews scheduled, public opportunities created, qualified job candidates contacted, and much more. Be sure to check them out to get a better idea of where you're at.

Focus on others' needs, not yours

There's a saying in marketing — "People don't care about your product; they only care about finding solutions to their own problems." This is a golden rule that every marketing expert will follow when marketing a particular product or service. They will tailor it in a way that shows the target audience how the product or service solves their problem effectively.

You must remember the exact same thing when it comes to LinkedIn etiquette, too. People don't care what you want or what you have to say. They will only pay attention to you if you have something of value to offer to them.

Profile Strategies

Be Public

We want to make sure your profile shows up when people search for you on the Internet. To do that, it's important to have the right profile settings on LinkedIn. Go to Privacy & Settings on your homepage, and from there, you can manage your profile settings. Click on Edit Your Public Profile button and see what items are shown there. You can choose which items you want visible to people using a public search. On the right side, you can see the items visible on your private profile.

Now, what things you decide to show to the public are completely up to you. Some people prefer going fully transparent and making all sections of their private profile visible publicly. That is okay. On the other hand, others choose to show only a few sections publicly, so as to give the viewer a brief overview. That's okay, too. Whatever you choose to do depends on the type of work you do and the degree of public visibility you're fine with.

One thing you need to remember is that rich-text media will never be visible in public searches, so full-text recommendations and videos are out of the picture. This is why your job experience and description are the most important parts of your profile. They attract the public viewer to check your full profile. Make sure this information is clear and interesting.

Custom profile URL

The last thing we touch upon in this process is your public profile URL. Your URL is unique to your profile, and you should use it tactically to further improve your profile's visibility. When you create a good profile URL, it gives your profile a boost in public search rankings. A higher-ranking profile will obviously be more visible, and you will get more hits.

And another cool little thing you can do with it is share it with your clients and others in your network, because it will be easy for them to remember and get in touch with you later.

Right Information is Key

Next, you'll need to see what your profile looks like to a stranger on the web. Log out of LinkedIn and search yourself on Google. Hopefully, if you have a name that's not too common, you'll see your own LinkedIn profile as one of the first few links on the Google search results. When you click on it, you'll see the public version of your profile that is visible to everyone. Once you see it, you can assess what looks good and what needs changing. There will definitely be some areas you can improve upon.

Here are some questions you need to ask yourself when looking at your public profile objectively:

- Is there any critical information missing from my public profile?

- Is there something I want my public profile to communicate that isn't being communicated right now?

- Is there an important message I am not giving to the public about my work?

- Could I benefit from showing something else

on my public profile?

Once you've asked yourself these questions, it's time to figure out the answers and write them down so you can use them later while editing your public profile. You will also have a rough structure and database of things you can add to your profile.

The next step is obviously opening your LinkedIn account and updating your profile. Check your job description, skills listed, and everything else that is important and publicly visible. You will have no difficulty tackling this since you already made a list of improvements to be incorporated.

Differentiate and capitalize

Now that your public profile is properly set up, you will start getting more attention from people in your industry who are looking for people of your expertise. But there's more to it than just getting people to view your profile — this is just the first step. You want people who look at your profile to ultimately connect with you. That is what benefits you, right?

So it's time to differentiate your private and public profile. Your private profile needs to offer even better content, so the viewer is pleased and impressed. This means there should be additional information in your private profile, like your recommendations and other rich-text media, which is top-notch. Take the example of someone who makes YouTube content as a part of their job. They can definitely benefit from sharing some of their best videos in their private profile.

You can even add photos and videos telling people about your work and experience. This not only increases the aesthetic value of your profile, but also encourages trust for your visitors. Don't forget to ask your friends and colleagues to write good recommendations for you, and do the same for them. This is a fantastic way to make your mark and stand out, because recommendations provide social proof of your competence — and human beings in general like social proof to help them make important decisions.

Search Engine Optimization

One of the biggest things in search engine optimization is the keyword. If you want any sort of content to be properly visible on the Internet, you need to include enough relevant keywords. This applies to your LinkedIn profile, too. For it to be highly visible in public searches, it must contain certain important keywords.

The first thing you need to do is use LinkedIn's search feature to look up the relevant keywords for your niche and create a list. As an example, using keywords like "sales" and "selling" is a good idea if sales is one of your primary skills.

The next step is to use these relevant keywords, one by one, and see how you rank in the search results. The further down you are in the results, the more improvements your profile needs. Look at the profiles of people who are higher up on the list and take note of this key area. Analyze how they've used important keywords to strengthen their profile, and learn from it.

The final step is to go to your own profile and edit it. Your goal is to add keywords as strategically as possible without sounding redundant. You can use these keywords in your headings, summary, and job description. This will improve the visibility of your profile across the platform and the Internet as a whole.

Go Premium

If you have the money to spare and really want a boost, consider going pro. With a premium plan of LinkedIn, you get a lot of new features.

Now that you've covered the basics and done everything to make your profile look good, what else can you do to make it even better? And yes, you can make it even better. There are certain things that make all the difference between a good and a great profile. In this chapter, we're going to take a look at some advanced tips for people who want to take to an even greater level and create a 5-star LinkedIn profile.

Support additional languages

Some jobs are localized and don't have to offer additional language support; however, some jobs can benefit from offering support for languages other than English. So, if you are someone who caters to an international clientele or industry and you often work with people from other countries, it's a good idea to make your profile available in multiple languages.

LinkedIn has many languages available, and you can choose any number of them. Create multiple versions of your profile in different languages, and make sure you have also updated the profile information with appropriately translated data. It will go a long way in getting you international connections.

In fact, your summary doesn't even have to be an exact translation. You can tweak it to cater to the demographics of different countries, if you know what they value most.

Rearrange sections

Many people are now aware that with LinkedIn, they can organize different sections of their profile to make it look how they please. This helps show off the prioritized stuff first. If you know what people in your industry look for first, you can bring those relevant sections to the top. Here are some of the sections in your profile you can rearrange:

- Projects
- Publications
- Certifications
- Summary
- Additional Info
- Organizations
- Experience
- Education
- Courses

Some people work in industries where prospective employers and clients don't care about where you went to school or how many degrees you have, so those people can put the Education section toward the end. It can be reversed for industries where this sort of information is important and relevant.

Check your profile on different platforms

We all know that Internet usage on mobile devices has increased manifold in the last few years because of the revolution in the telecom industry. According to the latest stats, more than 50% of users check LinkedIn via mobile, so it's important for you to take a look at how your profile appears on mobile devices.

You will obviously notice some changes, and you can correct these to ensure your profile looks great on every platform. Similarly, if you have embedded your profile anywhere, you should also check how it looks there. If you want LinkedIn Widgets, you can use these from the LinkedIn Plugins page. Make sure the Widgets you are using are both functional and attractive.

Regularly Publish Posts

Blogging on LinkedIn is still fairly new, but it's a powerful means to make a name for yourself and establish yourself as an influencer in your industry. If you churn out quality posts regularly, you will be seen as a thought leader. People will look up to you, and they will await your posts with eagerness.

Make sure you think of new topics to write about each week or two, and then research them to find lots of relevant data. Write a well-crafted post and publish it with a relevant, catchy image. This will surely get you attention from people in your industry, if you publish quality posts consistently. Make sure you stay away from easy, overly done topics that nobody cares about anymore. Quality trumps quantity every time.

With these tips, you will build an absolute powerhouse of a profile. Take some time out of your daily schedule and work on these things. The effort will pay off, I promise.

Chapter Four: YouTube

YouTube marketing is quite different from any other kind of marketing because it's entirely dependent on videos. You also have to dedicate far more time and energy into creating content that your subscribers will want to watch. It might be easy to get people to like and engage with a Facebook post, but making them watch your videos and follow your business is another ball game.

Before you turn on your camera and start blasting videos into the universe, take pause and think about why you're creating a YouTube channel and what your goals are. Building a channel can be a long, hard, uphill trudge, and if you are completely focused on numbers and analytics, it can be disheartening at times. (If your goal is just to make some quick cash through pre-roll ads, I can assure you, there are much easier and faster ways to make money online.)

Why Should You Create a YouTube Channel?

- Showcase your creativity?
- Make money?

- Meet people?
- Build a brand?
- Market your business?
- Tell a story?
- Promote a product?
- Showcase your work and get a job?
- Increase traffic to your blog or website?

YouTube is an amazing platform for all of these things, and all of them are legitimate reasons to start a channel.

However, if you aren't really into video games, don't start a video game channel just because PewDiePie is the biggest channel on YouTube right now.

For a great example of someone who has built a huge audience for a very niche passion, check out The Blu Collection. This channel is all about a guy's toy collection with a huge focus on toys based on the *Cars* movies. At the time of writing this, he has over 1 billion views and is adding almost 2,000 subscribers a day. I've only skimmed his channel, but he obviously loves what he is doing, and this has translated into a thriving audience.

The vast majority of shows on YouTube are created without even considering the potential audience. You can still find success, but taking time to think about your audience in advance can give your project an extra edge.

Ask yourself honestly:

- Will anybody really want to watch this show?
- If your answer is yes, who are they?
- Why are they going to watch?
- What is the best way to communicate with them?
- How are they going to find your show?
- How are you going to connect with them?

Ultimately, I think there is an audience for just about everything. But by thinking hard about who that audience is, you will be able to design a show that resonates with them more immediately, and you will find them faster.

When it comes to YouTube channels, it's better not to use the term audience. Instead, try to use the word community. Audience implies a one-way communication. Community involves not only two-way communication, but also something more complex. This is one of the things that really differentiate web shows and television shows. Don't make the mistake of being a narcissistic person — cultivate your community and treat your viewers with respect.

If you're a super creative person, you're probably going to want to reinvent the wheel on a regular basis. But trust me — you don't have time to do that. To build a loyal YouTube following, you need to produce videos on a consistent schedule. The more consistent, the better. I've tested just about every conceivable variation of upload schedule and frequency. Based on this testing, the most important factor seems to be consistency.

If you're doing something that is relatively simple from a production standpoint, I highly recommend designing a show that you can produce weekly. If you're producing something more ambitious — such as short films or animation — a consistent schedule is still important. If you can only produce one episode per month, determine a monthly schedule and stick with it.

Lots of people get hung up on all the equipment they think they need to get started. The truth is, you probably already have everything you need to at least start out. The camera quality on most smartphones is good enough, initially. There are very popular vlogs that are shot entirely with webcams. Instead of overthinking it, figure out how you can make the most out of what you've got. This applies to your content, as well. Build your show around locations, props, talent, and resources you have easy access to.

Your regular viewers (the foundation of your community) are not showing up every week to see your fancy camerawork — and many times, they're not even there for the topic of the video. They're showing up to see (and connect with) your on-camera personality. Design your format so that it spotlights and reflect that personality.

Setting up a YouTube Channel

Regardless of your purpose for creating a YouTube channel, it doesn't take much time to create one. After your channel has been created and approved, you can change its appearance, edit your videos if necessary, and perhaps group your videos into different playlists. Whether you are creating your YouTube account for your business or just want to start a personal brand, here is a simple 3-step checklist you can follow:

Create A Google Account

This is important, provided you didn't have one previously. By default, your YouTube username will be your Google username. Hence, when you upload your videos, this username is what everyone else sees. However, you are free to change it once you're on YouTube. If you have a Gmail account, you already have a Google account, and you have access to all Google products such as Google Play, Google Drive, and YouTube.

But before you can sign onto YouTube from your Google account, you will be asked to provide your first and last name. This is the name that will be used to identify you on YouTube. You can either choose a different name or use your actual first and last name.

The name of your YouTube channel, as you know, is very important. I would say the popular YouTubers are split almost equally between using their real name and a brand name. Now, this really depends on your preference for privacy and what your channel content is going to be about. For example, most vlogging channels tend to use their full name, whereas most gaming channels tend to use a brand or a made-up name. Be creative.

If your channel is going to be about an idea, concept, or a brand, then you're going to want to use the brand name. Coming up with a brand name is something you should think about long and hard. A few tips that you can mix and match:

- Alliteration e.g., "Charisma on Command."
- Wordplay/ Rhyming e.g., "PewDiePie."
- A single word e.g., "Vsauce."

That being said, your channel name isn't overly important as long as the content is quality. For example, most cannot even pronounce the channel name "Kurzgesagt," however; their videos consistently pull millions of views. Pick a name you like and are passionate about, and stick with it. Once you have filled these required fields, select "Create Channel."

Customize the appearance of your channel

The first impression of your channel is extremely important. Of course, the quality of your videos is supreme above all the rest; however, the truth is, it's best to cover all your bases.

Some of the most important things that you should customize are:

- Channel's icon
- Channel's art
- Channel's description

If you want to update these basic things, head on over to your channels, and you'll see an edit button next to whatever you want to change — just click on it.

Channel Icon

This should be an interesting photo of yourself, professional, or even taken on an iPhone. The main purpose of this photo is to draw people to click on your channel, so try and make it eye-catching. A scientifically-based trick is to include your face in the icon (if appropriate) and pull a face that's related to your YouTube channel (check out Vsauce's icon) or just use a picture of you smiling.

You can also use your channel name as inspiration for the logo. If you're really stuck, you can go on the website fiverr.com and get a high-quality logo made for as little as $5. You can also get your pictures professionally edited to include your logo on them here. People also opt for drawn versions of themselves, and this can be really good, especially if you're not the most photogenic (like me).

Channel Art

As mentioned previously, you can get a nice banner made for as low as $5 on Fiverr, or you can use free stock photos from pexels.com or use any wallpaper you like. This is not such an important part of your channel, and you can perhaps use this to advertise a book you've released or place a link to your website.

Channel description

This part of your channel is important. Although the amount of people that check your channel description in relation to your subscribers is going to be fairly low, it's good to include links to any other social media profiles you want to share, as well as links to your website. Many YouTubers also include a FAQ for questions you might be asked a lot. A crucial thing, if needed, is to include a business email. Don't use your personal email. This can be extremely useful for increasing the revenue you make on YouTube, and we'll go into detail on this later in the book.

You can also add a featured channels section and add

a trailer to your channel. A channel trailer is important, as it lets people know what they can expect to see from you. Here, what I would do is feature my most popular/ best video, in order to get the best possible early impression of my channel. You can also change how the videos are laid out and also enable 'channel comments' under the discussion section. Any change you desire to make can be done by clicking the settings icon next to your subscribe button. Next, click on the "customize the layout of your channel" option.

Start uploading your videos

To get access to the upload page, first, you have to log in and press the 'upload' button. You can find this button on the right-top side of the YouTube site.

When you want to upload your videos, you can:

- Drag videos to the upload page,
- Click the large upload area to browse for videos from your PC, or
- Press the 'import' button that you will find next to the 'import videos' side, to the right of the upload screen. With this, you can upload photos from your computer or even Google photos.

You can also try making a slideshow using photos.

This is available on the right-hand side of the upload page.

Pro tip: make sure you select either public, unlisted, private, or scheduled as it suits you when you want to upload videos from your PC. When you make your videos public, anyone can see them. When they are unlisted, only those who have a direct link can access the video. When they are private, only you can see it, and you have to be logged in before you can see them. When you want to schedule your videos, you can set the time when they will be available to the public.

Other factors you need to keep in mind:

If your browser is up to date, the video you want to upload should have a maximum size of 128 GB. Otherwise, you will only be able to upload a video with a maximum size of 20 GB. Your video editing software should give you a good idea of how big your video is before you render it — most of the time, it's rare to exceed 20 GB.

Unless you verify your YouTube account, your videos cannot exceed 15 minutes in length. Once you have verified your YouTube account, this limit is removed. This is good to keep in mind, depending on the type of content you want to make.

Make sure your videos are in mp4 format when you want to upload them. If not, you will get an "invalid file format" error. However, you can convert your video to an acceptable format; I would recommend Adobe Premiere or Sony Vegas Pro for this purpose.

These are paid software, of which free alternatives are Windows Movie Maker (I would, however, not recommend this solution).

You can use YouTube's video editor to add titles, captions, split the video into clips, add photos, and make video transitions. Read more on exactly how to edit your video later.

If you want to manage your videos easily, arrange them into custom playlists.

Creating YouTube Videos

Over the past few years, some major production companies have launched big-budget productions on YouTube. We saw a lot of these when YouTube was doling out millions to fund original content. Many of them have taken a traditional television approach to the style. Big budgets, amazing videography, aggressive editing, and even some mid-list "stars" have characterized these productions. There were a few successes, but the majority of them failed. In my opinion, they failed because they were just making "TV" for YouTube, rather than recognizing the unique opportunities offered by the platform.

In theatre, there is the concept of a "fourth wall." The fourth wall is the invisible fourth wall at the front of a traditional three-walled box set. This is how the audience "sees" into the world of the play. When an actor acknowledges the existence of the audience, it's referred to as "breaking the fourth wall." This concept exists in the world of film and television, as well. In YouTube, the fourth wall is pretty much always broken. The most popular YouTube personalities talk directly to their audience. Some of the biggest recent scripted hits have come from Pemberley Digital (Lizzie Bennet Diaries) who have built their entire company on a broken fourth wall. They've now produced several incredibly successful stories that all are essentially characters talking into a webcam.

When watching videos on YouTube, there is always the sense that a person made the video, or at least liked a video enough to upload it. Your viewers want a sense of connection and relationship with you. Embrace this, rather than obscuring it with fancy editing or flashy graphics that will look outdated next year.

There is no perfect format for a video. There is no ideal length. There is no magic recipe that works every time for every video. The only way to get close is to get started, pay attention to the response (analytics), and then make tweaks to improve what you're doing. That being said, here are a few tips to use as a starting point:

Format

Opening

A quick introduction that tells you exactly what you're going to see in the video. For food videos, make sure to get a shot of the finished dish in the first 10 seconds. Ideally, end it with a joke — or something that provides a good lead-in to the intro music.

Title / Intro

An introductory sequence with some music and the title — try to evoke the overall feel for the show. Keep it short, 7 seconds or less.

The Meat

Time has really been of the essence in everything up to this point. Now, we can slow down and get into the video itself. The pacing is determined by the subject matter. Towards the end of this section, use annotations and a spoken call-to-action to ask the viewer to subscribe or recommend another video they might be interested in. I'd rather have them jump to another one of our videos than to go searching for something else.

End Card

This end card continues the branding that we established in the title/intro, but has at least one call to action — if not several. If someone has made it this far into the video, they are either already invested in your show, or very interested. This is a great chance to give them something to do next. Send them to another one of your videos or to the main website. Once you've launched a few videos, you can go to Video Retention in Analytics and see how things are working.

See if you can pinpoint when people are bailing on your video. If people are bouncing off at the very beginning, it may be time to go back to square one. However, if you get a big drop-off at 4:30, take a look and see what's happening in the middle of your videos. We will discuss analytics in detail later on in the book.

Gear

If you're going to produce a show, you're going to need a little bit of equipment. It's really easy to get hung up on this point and spend endless hours on camera websites and forums doing "research." Cameras are so good right now and camera technology is evolving so quickly that you really are just wasting time. By the time your camera arrives, something new and better will be announced.

Instead, just find something that works for you and your project and start shooting. What you need will depend on what kind of show you're going to make. Conversely, if you don't have a budget, the type of show you can make will depend on the gear you have.

If you have an iPhone, you could invest in a few inexpensive accessories and apps to shoot high-quality footage. A new phone from Samsung even shoots 4K video.

At a bare minimum, here are the things you will need:

Camera

The release of the Canon 5D MKII started a revolution that completely blurred the line between video cameras and still cameras. Some of the best video quality is now coming from DSLR cameras.

Image quality is, of course, incredibly important, but the audio quality is even more so. You've got to have a way to plug a microphone into your camera. You could sync the sound from an external recorder later, but that adds time in post-production. For most people, having an audio input jack is a much simpler solution.

Based on conversations and research around the

YouTube community this year, the Canon Rebel series (T3i, T4i, T5i) seems to be the current go-to camera for YouTubers. The camera I would recommend is the T3i — it's got a flip-out monitor, audio input jack, and even has the same image sensor as a 60D.

YouTube superstar iJustine posted an Instagram photo showing her vlogging cameras with the following caption: "It all has to fit in my purse :) GoPro for all those quick wide-angle shots. Canon XA10 when you need a mic input and autofocus + lots of zooms! Pink Canon SD960 = best vlogging camera — perfect audio for concerts and windy settings, quick focus! Canon S110 — better video quality than 960, audio peaks if it's too loud and you can hear the autofocus lens in playback. The mic is on the front so if it's windy, don't even bother — it's best for b-roll and photos! The end."

If you're interested in going the iPhone route, I highly recommend the online course "iPhone Video Hero" by Jules Watkins. Ultimately, your camera is just a tool. Everybody has their favorite tools, and certain tools work better for certain situations. Start with a camera you already have or find one that you can afford (ideally with a mic input!) and get shooting. If you're looking for a place to start:

ENTRY LEVEL DSLR: Canon T5i

Cost: Around $1,000 with the kit lens. If you want to save even more money, you could buy a used T3i, which is essentially the same camera. Or look for a T2i, which is basically the same but without a flip-out screen. However, the flip-out screen will always come in handy.

MID-RANGE VIDEO CAMERA: Canon XA20

Cost: Around $2,000. This camera is used a lot around the YouTube space and almost everybody shoots with it. If you want to save a little money, look for the XA10, which is a nearly identical older model. Both of these cameras have a convenient detachable handle that mounts on the top to give you XLR audio inputs and manual audio controls. These cameras also have cool infrared features that you can use if you're into that kind of thing.

ENTRY LEVEL PRO: Canon C100

Cost: $5,000. In my opinion, the Canon Cinema line continues the DSLR revolution. These cameras keep a lot of the great features and image quality we got from DSLRs, but bring back the features we'd been missing from video cameras: manual audio controls, focus peaking, waveforms, long record times, no overheating.

Microphone

Never underestimate the power of good audio. Don't risk missteps in this department, and always look for ways to improve. The on-camera mic is not going to cut it.

If your videos feature a lot of talking-head stuff in controllable locations, I highly recommend you pick up a wired lavalier mic. Do a search on Amazon and you can find decent ones as low as $20. You can also upgrade to the Sennheiser Evolution G3 wireless mic system.

Another popular choice in the YouTube community is the Rode VideoMic Pro. This is a microphone that mounts to your camera and does a pretty good job of picking up whatever sounds are directly in front of it. It's not ideal, but it is better than trying to use the on-camera mic.

There are a lot of affordable options for getting decent sound, but — unlike with cameras — this is an area where spending more money really does make a huge difference in quality.

Something To Stabilize Your Camera

You're going to need something to keep your camera steady — nobody wants to see shaky handheld footage. A tripod is your best bet. These can range from under ten dollars to tens of thousands of dollars. If your budget is really low, you can probably find a used tripod at a garage sale. You won't be able to do smooth camera movements with it, but it will hold your camera still.

The Lollipod ($50-60) is an excellent entry-level tripod that is also designed to work as a monopod or light stand. These are lightweight and fold down really small, making them great for travel. Add on a Glif tripod mount or Universal Phone Holder and you will be all set to shoot great video with your phone.

As the name implies, a monopod is a one-legged camera support. These are great for travel and event shooting where you need to move fast but want to avoid shaky footage.

Lights (maybe)

If you are going to be shooting outdoors or have a "set" with lots of natural light, you might be able to get away with no additional lights. However, most people are going to need a simple light setup.

Basic Lighting Kit

Cowboy Studio makes inexpensive light kits. They come in lots of different configurations, but you can usually get a kit with three softbox lights from around $250. I recommend compact fluorescent Daylight Balanced photo bulbs — they stay pretty cool and will match the daylight from any nearby windows. The build quality is not great on these kits so don't expect them to last forever, but they will get you up and running and, at this price, you can easily replace any pieces that break.

LED Lights

These are more expensive but can be a lot of fun to work with. Litepanels are a good option, as they are high in quality and reasonably priced, as opposed to most other brands. Lights and related gear can get very expensive very quickly. My suggestion is to start with the bare minimum and see if you can make it work, then upgrade only when you really need to. If you have your eye on something expensive, rent it and try it out before you buy it.

Editing

Fear (or hatred) of editing is probably the second biggest obstacle to getting your YouTube channel up and running. I hear from people all the time about how much they dislike editing, and I've never really understood it.

During production, just about anything can go wrong and there are often elements you have no control over. But once you're in post-production, you can focus on what you've got. It's your chance to take all that footage you shot and sculpt and polish it into a finished piece that your audience will love. The software has gotten so good, it's almost as easy to edit videos as it is to make a PowerPoint presentation. For this stage, you're going to need a computer and some editing software. Once again, there are no excuses —

you can edit video on an iPhone or iPad now. Most computers come with some sort of free editing software. On Mac, you'll have iMovie. On Window, it's MovieMaker. If you don't like those, you've now got more choices than ever.

Screenflow

As the name implies, the primary purpose of Screenflow is screen recording. If you're doing any type of software demonstration videos, or you just want to show what's happening on your computer screen, you need to get Screenflow. Over time, ScreenFlow has developed a surprisingly robust set of editing features. It's gotten so good that some video creators use Screenflow exclusively. If your show has a relatively simple format (vlogs, product demonstration, fitness videos), Screenflow could be the perfect tool for the job. It's got a great interface for editing audio and video tracks, and comes packed with easy-to-use titles and transitions. If you're on a budget (and on a Mac), grab a copy of ScreenFlow and get to work.

Final Cut Pro X

FCPX is probably the most controversial editing software ever. Apple's overhaul of the much-loved Final Cut Pro was not received well by the editing community and has fallen out of grace with the majority of professional editors. That being said, it's still one of the best software out there.

The interface is particularly well-suited to short-form content. FCPX has several core features that can take some getting used to if you're familiar with other Non-Linear Editors. One of its key differentiating features is the magnetic timeline. Instead of a bunch of different tracks that are all of equal importance, FCPX uses the concept of a storyline. It's almost like a tube that you put the clips into in the order you want them to appear in the finished piece. Then, FCPX automatically fills in the gaps.

You can also throw just about any type of footage into FCPX and the software will figure out what to do with it. There are very few pop-up windows asking you to supply information. Just import the footage and get started. Apple has released free updates for FCPX every couple of months and some of them have included some pretty massive new features. If you haven't checked it out in a while, it might be time to give it another look.

Adobe Premiere

Adobe Premiere has picked up the gauntlet from Final Cut Pro 7 and become the NLE of choice for many professional editors. It's only available as part of the Adobe Creative Cloud, so there is a monthly subscription fee. However, as part of the subscription, you gain access to all of the Adobe Creative Suite, which includes essentials like Photoshop and Audition.

If your project will have lots of motion graphics generated by Adobe After Effects, Premiere should definitely be your top choice. This is a big application and it does a lot. If you've never edited before, there will be a learning curve, but once you get up and running, you won't regret having learned it.

Post-Production

There are a lot of steps involved in post-production. Here's a super-simplified post-production workflow:

1. Import Footage
2. Edit Footage
3. Add Transitions and Text
4. Customize End Card
5. Add Music
6. Balance Audio Levels
7. Color Correct Footage
8. Add Intro Title Sequence

Some of those steps may only take a few minutes, but

they add up. Especially when you are doing each step for a new video every week. As you're making your videos, think about what would happen if you had to delegate the task of post-production to somebody else. Would it be possible to make a checklist that someone else could follow to successfully produce an episode? It sounds like the opposite of creativity, but you will find that having a solid system in place directly helps you produce work more quickly — allowing you to feel much more satisfied creatively.

Strategies for YouTube

In this section, we will look at some great strategies that will help increase user engagement with your YouTube videos:

Cards and End Screens

YouTube recently did away with Annotations in favor of Cards and End Screens and, when used properly, these new tools can dramatically increase engagement and subscription rates for your channel. Let's take a look at each one and discuss how they work and best practices for using them effectively.

Cards

Cards are calls-to-action that can be added anywhere

in your video in order to push viewers to watch a different video or playlist of yours, navigate to a different channel altogether, click a link, donate, or participate in a poll. You can add up to five of these to a single video.

You have to be careful with how you use Cards, though. If used improperly, they can lead to decreased watch time on your videos, since you're basically giving the user an exit! Luckily, when a user clicks a card, it opens in a new window and pauses the current video, but this could still increase your video attrition rate since the user may just end up closing the original video.

Don't be afraid to experiment and find what works best for your channel. You can monitor the performance of your Cards in YouTube's Analytics — just go to your "Creator Studio", click "Analytics" in the sidebar, then click "Cards".

One final tip with cards is to promote playlists over individual videos. If you are specifically trying to drive traffic to a single video, that's fine. But playlists have the added benefit of auto-playing so, theoretically, your viewer is more likely to watch more than just one video.

End Screens

End screens are simply calls-to-action that you can overlay during the last 20 seconds of a video in order to encourage the user to engage in some way.

Before End Screens came on the scene, creators had to manually add annotations to the end of every video. This was a tedious process and didn't look very aesthetically pleasing. Plus, annotations aren't mobile-friendly, so that call-to-action (CTAs) was basically lost if the viewer was on their phone. And considering more than half of all YouTube views come from mobile, that's kind of a big deal.

The End Screen tool makes all of this much easier by providing a standard tool for adding calls-to-action to the end of your video. It also displays on mobile, which is a huge benefit.

In addition to a subscribe CTA and Patreon CTA, I suggest including a link to another video in order to entice the user to keep on watching. YouTube has a handy feature where you can select a specific video to show, or you can have it determine the best video based on the viewer's prior behavior. You can also promote playlists here.

Keep it Short

During the editing process, think like a Ninja and cut anything that doesn't add to the story. As a creator, you might feel that everything you shoot is important, but you've got to be ruthless with what goes and what stays. If your first draft edit is 10 minutes long, see if you can shorten scenes or remove them entirely to get it down to 8 minutes or 5 minutes.

Provide value to the viewer

If your video is informative in nature, stick to the most powerful points and describe them in a brief manner. This will help the content move along quickly, ensuring the viewer doesn't get bored. If your video is more entertainment-based, keep the scenes and story moving and maintain the energy up throughout the video. As a rule of thumb, try not to stay on the same scene for more than 10 seconds.

Show your brand

After the intro is a great opportunity to show off your brand. Many creators opt to insert a fancy animation (once again, Fiverr is a great site for getting those on the cheap); others create their own short brand sequence just to show who they are.

Search Magnets

YouTube ranks as the 2nd most widely-used search engine, world-wide. It might seem like if you rank well in YouTube you'd also rank well in Google, but that's not the case. When it comes to optimizing your content for search engines, we're all playing a guessing game, to a certain extent. Google offers occasional hints about what works, but the algorithm is top secret. All we can do is experiment, share our knowledge, and guess some more. The YouTube search engine shares some characteristics with Google, but the current YouTube algorithm seems to be a lot simpler and much easier to crack. For this book, our focus is on ranking well on YouTube.

The following are what I believe to be the 5 Key Factors that determine how videos rank in the YouTube Search Engine (until they change it).

Title and Metadata

They're getting closer, but as of the time of this writing, YouTube can't accurately index video content. Take a look at the default captions sometime, if you don't believe me. The automated transcripts are usually pretty hilarious. Since the algorithm doesn't know what your video is about, you're going to have to tell it. The easiest way is through carefully filling out your title, description, and tags. If you neglect this step, the algorithm doesn't even know where to start. You can take this to the next level by transcribing your videos and adding text captions.

Titles and Metadata are particularly important in the first 48 hours after launching your video. At this stage, YouTube doesn't have any user data, so take advantage of this critical window. After the first 48 hours, Watch Time becomes the priority.

Watch Time

How long are viewers actually watching the videos? YouTube has officially stated that this is one of the most important factors they take into account when ranking a video. If people are bouncing off your videos within the first 30 seconds, the YouTube algorithm is going to take that as a sign that this is not a very good video (or that people are not finding what they are looking for). You can improve watch time by structuring your videos in a way that is engaging, making great thumbnails and accurately describing the video in the title, description, and tags.

Likewise, if a significant amount of viewers are spending a lot of time watching the video that sends a signal that this is good quality content. YouTube also pays attention to Session Time. This is the overall time a user is spending on YouTube during a session. If your video leads viewers to another video (even if it's not on your channel), your channel will get partial credit. YouTube wants people to stick around on the site and watch lots of videos (and ads). If your videos promote longer overall session times, this will help boost their rankings.

Subscribers

Subscriber count is still important because the more subscribers you have, the faster you can get views and comments, so it ties into everything else. The first 48 hours are incredibly important and the more active and engaged subscribers you have, the easier it is to rack up a bunch of views quickly every time a video launches.

Comments

Comments show that the video is "alive" and that people are not only watching it, but also interacting with it. It always surprises me when people turn off comments; they are shooting themselves in the foot when it comes to generating traffic. YouTube comments can be incredibly annoying, but take them with a grain of salt and be proactive about responding.

One of the positive things about YouTube comments is the ability to blacklist certain words in your comment settings. If abusive comments are bringing you down, use this setting to filter out recurring offensive words. You can also ban trolls as they pop up. The system is far from perfect, but it's much better than it used to be. And dealing with a few negative comments is worth it for the positive effect commenting in general can bring to your channel.

Backlinks

Backlinks are links that point to your video, and they are one of the most important factors in SEO. Search engines see these links as "votes," which tell the robots that the content being linked to is legitimate and is what it says it is.

This was a fairly easy system to scam prior to 2009.

If you had a video or blog post about "How To Fly a Kite," all you needed was a properly optimized post and more links than anybody else to be ranked #1. You could buy backlink packages on Fiverr and rank really well for pretty much anything. Google has gotten a lot more sophisticated at detecting these kinds of schemes, and YouTube is getting there, as well.

You can still build a legitimate web of links to your videos without doing anything shady. Look for areas on your platform to add relevant links. Links from other videos (in descriptions and annotations) and curated playlists are great places. You don't want your video to exist in isolation.

You may notice a few recurring themes here: indicators of quality and social signals. If you're making great videos, most of these will come naturally.

Keywords

Before we go further, let's take a look at an essential concept called keywords. It can be quite confusing, but it's really just an industry term used to explain how the words you use in your videos are the key to attracting an audience.

When anyone searches for anything on Google or any other search engine, the specific words they use to search are called keywords. Some words are so frequently and widely used, they become popular keywords. If your site has the right keywords, you can boost your ranking on Google search to easily attract customers.

Keywords are important, but they are just that — words. You don't have to care about how your content matches with them. So, don't let keywords impact how you create or display content, and just add relevant keywords after you're done creating. People search specific words because they are looking for a video that matches the idea of those words. Look at the problem your site or video is trying to solve, and imagine what words a person could possibly type if they were looking for that particular solution. Add those keywords to make sure that, for that specific problem, Google would direct searchers to your site.

Keyword Research

Once you start thinking about Search Engine Optimization, you will realize how important it can be for your business. Don't fall into the trap of tutorial videos that promise false results — focus instead on keywords, because that's all it takes to get people to your site. Keyword research should only add a few minutes to your production time for each video.

Now, we're going to look at an example of how you can use the technique of Keyword Research. The example is of a video about poaching eggs.

- Start the Google AdWords Keyword Planner — It's free, but you have to sign up for an

AdWords account.

- Click "Search For New Keywords and Group Ideas" — Type a few words and phrases into the "Your Product or Service" box.

- Under "Customize Your Search >> Keyword Options", check the box for "Only Show Options Closely Related to My Search" — This will help keep your search narrowed down.

- Click "Get Ideas"

- Evaluate the Keywords — The tool will give you a list of potential keywords and will indicate how many people use each keyword monthly. You'll also notice a column for Competition. The Competition ranking is not about how hard it will be to outrank the other terms; instead, it refers to how competitive the term is when it comes to buying paid AdWords ads. Don't let a high competition scare you off. That just means the ads running on your video will bring in more money.

- Pick the words you want to capture – In this scenario, it seems like many people search for "how to poach an egg," so let's try to target that. You should also try to chance upon other words that Google is showing. Try to use keywords that have fewer hits and limited competitors.

By just taking a few minutes to check the Google

Keyword Tool, we've discovered that "how to poach an egg" has the potential to bring in a lot more traffic than "how to poach eggs" or "poached eggs". They're all an accurate description of the video, so let's target the one that potentially will bring in more viewers.

If you have a keyword or phrase in mind before you shoot your video, work that keyword into the dialog of the video in a natural way. This will give you an extra edge if you have your videos transcribed and captioned.

Strategies for Engagement

Your channel is what sells your videos to people, and it needs to entice your target audience until they're interested enough to watch your uploads. In this section, we will look at the most important tips for running a YouTube Channel.

The first step, of course, is to make sure that every aspect of your channel is refined and every little thing is taken care of. So, here's how you can sell your brand with your channel:

Create an eye-catching YouTube banner

One thing that most successful YouTubers have in common is that they all have interesting and well thought-out channel banners. After all, it's the first thing the viewers see when they land on your page. Now, you might be thinking, "But I'm not a designer," or, "I don't have money for professional photos." Well, believe it or not, it's actually possible to create an eye-catching, well-designed channel banner for next to nothing — and you don't have to be a professional designer to do it.

First, let's talk about what makes a good channel banner. The best banners are very simple — they typically rely on a solid background color or a subtle gradient, which helps ensure that the imagery and message stand out.

A good banner also explains the purpose of your channel. Whether your content is about business, travel, gaming, home décor, or whatever else, the goal of your channel should be clearly stated in your banner in as few words as possible.

Lastly, a good banner fits your brand. It should follow a similar color scheme to other assets of your brand like your avatar, website, business cards, and so on.

One thing to keep in mind when designing your channel banner is that YouTube shows your banner at different sizes depending on what device the viewer is on, whether it's the desktop, mobile, or tablet app.

There are also plenty of free graphics programs out there that you can use to design your awesome banner. Canva is a great browser-based app that makes it easy to design YouTube banners, as well as social media posts, business cards, presentations, and more. There's also GIMP and Vectr, which are a bit more complicated to use but are also completely free.

Channel Trailer

Another area where new YouTubers fail to maximize the platform is with their channel trailer. Your channel trailer works just like the trailer for a movie — it explains what your channel is all about and what the viewer can expect to see if they subscribe. It's one of the most important aspects of your YouTube channel for converting viewers to subscribers. Here's a guide you can use for creating a solid channel trailer:

- Start with a warm introduction. Introduce yourself to your future viewers, tell them who you are and where you're from. Don't be afraid to show off your personality!

- Explain what viewers can expect to see if they subscribe to your channel and how often you upload new videos. Upload schedules are extremely important and keep viewers coming back.

- Don't forget to ask the viewer to subscribe! After all, that's the whole point of the trailer, right?

- Keep your trailer short and sweet. Some trailers are 20-30 seconds long, others are 1-2 minutes — they are rarely longer than that. Remember, this may be the viewer's first encounter with your channel, so your trailer should be short, informative, and full of personality!

Create Playlists

Playlists are basically collections of videos that you collect under a single category. Once you've got a few playlists, you can organize them on your channel page for viewers to browse through, almost like flipping through TV shows.

Another important aspect of playlists is that when one video ends, the next one auto-plays. This means that when a viewer starts watching a playlist, they are more likely to keep on watching after a video ends, rather than just closing the page.

Having playlists on your channel also helps you seem more established, because it feels like you have a lot of content to choose from. But make sure you give each one a descriptive title, as well as a description that's chock full of keywords you'd like to target. This will help potential viewers find it! We'll talk more about Search Engine Optimization and how easy but powerful it is a little later.

Fill out your About Section & Channel Keywords

Your channel's about section gives you another opportunity to explain what your channel is all about. I recommend keeping this to only two or three powerful sentences, and don't be afraid to add a dash of personality! You can also use this section to explain your upload schedule and ask viewers to subscribe to your channel.

You can add keywords to your channel, as well, which can help users to discover your YouTube channel when they search for results on Google, YouTube, and other search engines.

Channel Watermark

Your branding watermark is a small image that sits at the bottom right of your videos. When new viewers hover over this watermark, they see a big subscribe button. Many YouTubers put their logo or avatar down here, but we've opted to put a "subscribe" graphic on ours so it's a little more obvious what this watermark is for.

Software Tools

Here's a little secret weapon that all the YouTube

pros are using: Tools. Once you start using these tools, you will get a huge leg up on the competition, because it will enable you to see things like revenue projections of other channels, subscriber growth, future growth predictions, and a ton of other things. These apps can also help you when posting your videos by providing insight into keywords, title, and cross-promotion you can use to maximize views and search engine optimization. Some even help you earn real money!

Before you do anything else, take a look at these tools and what they offer. They are all (mostly) free and can really take your YouTube game to the next level.

VidIQ

VidIQ can be installed as an add-on for Chrome or Firefox browsers and gives you immediate access to detailed stats on any video or channel page.

Having the VidIQ extensions is like having superpowers. It allows you to analyze any video (including your own) to see how much money it makes, how much it's been shared on other social networks, how well it's optimized for search, and much more. There is one drawback, however: it is a bit of a behemoth and will cause pages to load a bit slower.

In addition, VidIQ adds a ton of useful information to your YouTube search results page. You can use it to help you find new keywords to target and to see who your competition is.

VidIQ also adds useful tools to your video upload page, like recommended tags and similar videos. This is really useful because it often suggests tags you hadn't thought of, and the similar videos section offers a great opportunity for cross promoting. The thinking is that if you include the same tags and keywords, then you are more likely to appear in the suggested videos sidebar next to that similar video.

The free version only provides basic tag and video suggestions, but if you want to unlock all the power of VidIQ, consider upgrading to a paid plan. Basically, if you're using YouTube without this add-on, you're doing it wrong.

TubeBuddy

TubeBuddy is similar to VidIQ and offers quite a few of the same features, so I won't hash them all out again. I recommend trying both and deciding for yourself which one is the most helpful and loads the quickest.

SocialBlade

SocialBlade isn't an add-on, but it's an absolutely essential tool to include in your YouTube arsenal.

This site ranks all YouTube channels and provides detailed insights into their growth and future growth potential. It even guesses at their potential monthly revenue, though it's very much a generalized figure.

You can use SocialBlade to get a handy comparison on how your channel stacks up to others in your niche. This will give you an idea of how you're growing in relation to other successful channels, or channels that are around your size.

You can also use SocialBlade's future projections to get a sense of how you can expect your channel to grow in the future. Just keep in mind that this is very generalized information and will change drastically based on the actual growth of your channel, but they at least give you a ballpark idea.

If this seems like a lot to process, here are some examples of how you can use SocialBlade:

- Comparing your channel to others in order to decide if collaboration would be beneficial for both parties.

- To see how your channel will grow in the future, in order to better pitch potential brand partnerships.

- To compare your growth to the growth of larger channels in your similar niche. This will give you an idea of if you are on a similar track or not.

Gleam

Running contests and giveaways on your channel can be a great way to increase views and subscribers, and Gleam is an excellent tool for doing just that. It provides an interface for users to enter your contest or giveaway with a single click and gives you comprehensive tools for tracking entries, sharing your contest, and picking winners.

Famebit

Famebit is a service that connects creators to brands who are seeking partnerships. These can be in exchange for a product or for a fee. Currently, you need at least 5,000 subscribers in order to join Famebit as a creator.

YouTube Creator Studio

YouTube offers a handy little app for your phone called the YouTube Creator Studio, which gives you access to all of your channel analytics and details on the go. This app is an absolute must-have for any YouTube creator. It makes responding to and managing comments much easier, allows you to organize your videos and playlists, and gives you access to analytics insights that are harder to find on the web version of YouTube. And, best of all, it's free!

YouTube Analytics

In this section, we'll be looking at an important analytic tool for increasing your engagement and revenue – Analytics.

This part of YouTube typically sends new creators running for the hills, and for good reason. The Analytics tab in your creator dashboard can be a daunting button to press, since when you do, you're faced with charts, graphs, and tons of sub-sections. But allow me to put your mind at ease — analytics is actually really easy to understand, as long as you know what to look for.

When you start a new channel and load up your analytics dashboard, there isn't going to be much there. So, before you can start drawing conclusions from your analytics data, you've got to get some views on your channel. In the previous chapter, we discussed how to drive initial traffic to your page, so if you haven't already put those steps into place, do those now!

Once you've been able to get at least a few hundred views, you can start checking into your analytics to see what you can find. But one important thing to keep in mind is that YouTube Analytics data is delayed, which means that you won't see channel data as it happens, but about two days later. Keep in mind that anything you're seeing in your analytics dashboard is missing the last two days of data.

There is, however, a real-time section in the YouTube Analytics Dashboard, which will give you stats on the last 24 hours of views. This data is more limited than historical data, but it can give you an idea of how a video is performing, right this moment, and where your recent views are coming from.

Watch Time

In recent years, YouTube has been tweaking its algorithm to focus more on watch time. Watch time can be defined as the number of minutes that a viewer spends while watching a video. So, if you have a channel with 10-minute videos, but generally users only watch half of this, the average watch time can be said to be 5 minutes, or basically 50%.

For YouTube, a channel with a higher watch time means more revenue, because the channel can clearly hold viewers' attention. Most importantly, it's actually about the number of minutes that are being watched rather than the percentage of a video. For example, say there's a channel that has a 75% watch time on an average. If the videos on the channel are short, only 2 minutes long, then even though viewers might be watching most of the video, it's still not a lot of minutes.

Some YouTubers came up with a clever solution to this problem — they started making videos that were far longer than normal. This has definitely reduced the quality of the videos on YouTube since they are just showing the same content in a longer time, instead of adding any extra value. Most people just add content to their videos for no reason but to stretch the upload. At the end of the day, though, it's helping YouTube make more money, and hence helping you make money, too.

Watch time percentage is not completely useless, either, as compared to, say, the total watch time. You should always aim to increase your percentage watch time because, at the end of the day, it means viewers are seeing more of your videos. This is why you should continuously monitor this metric.

I believe that 50% watch time, in general, is a good mark to shoot for on any given video. So, if your videos are 6 minutes long, you should aim for a Watch Time of 3 minutes.

One way to improve your watch time is to experiment with tweaking your video format and content quality. The goal is to make your videos more useful, which is one of the best things you can do to improve watch time. You can also try to incorporate cliffhangers. We'll often mention something really fun we're going to do later on in the video, with the hope that it will entice viewers to stick around to see it.

Other Metrics to Watch

Watch time may be the most important metric, but it's not the only one you should be tracking. Here's a list of the most important metrics to keep up with in your Analytics dashboard:

Watch time/video length

As we've already discussed, the more a viewer is watching, the more effective a video is — and YouTube rewards that.

Subscriber to view ratio

This is an indication of how engaging your videos are to your subscriber base. If you have 1,000 subscribers and a video gets 100 views, that's a 10% subscriber to view ratio. In my opinion, you should aim for a minimum of 10%, but you can also try to shoot for 20 or 30%.

Video views in the first 24 to 48 hours

This also indicates how engaged your subscribers are and how quickly your video begins ranking in search. One great way to increase this is to push your subscribers to enable notifications. This ensures they get a push notification on their phone as soon as you upload a new video. Mention this in your videos and even demonstrate exactly how to do it to encourage subscribers to take advantage of the feature.

Traffic sources

How are people finding your video? If you know, then you can try to exploit that source to increase traffic even more. Some traffic sources are a bit cryptic. What the heck are "Browse features" and "YouTube channels," anyway? There's a handy guide from YouTube that explains what each one is, which you can find online.

Traffic locations

Your content might be resonating more with a specific country. Make sure you monitor geographic traffic sources in analytics too. If your content is resonating with people in Central America, for example, it might be worth it to translate your videos into Spanish or make specific videos for that audience.

Your most popular videos

Always look for which videos have the highest total views and daily views and try to figure out why these videos are doing so well.

You can find these front and center under the "Overview" section of your Analytics dashboard. Once you've identified your most successful videos, start digging into their individual analytics and look at their traffic sources, watch time, like / comment rate and more in order to see if you can uncover any patterns that you can replicate.

Collaborating

This is an area that can lead to huge growth for your channel, but it's also sometimes difficult to pull off. Collaboration is simply when two YouTubers come together to make a video. They typically create separate videos for each channel and promote each other's videos on their individual social media outlets once posted. Collaborating with other YouTubers does a few specific things that can lead to some big-time growth:

1. It exposes you to a new audience: Collaborating with a YouTuber who has an engaged subscriber base means you are

exposed to their viewers who have a high likelihood of subscribing to your channel. Even if the channel is smaller than you are, if their subscribers have high engagement, a collaboration could be worth it.

2. It builds your network: Teaming up with other YouTubers is a great way to make contacts and, more importantly, friends!

3. It gets you used to working with others: Thinking about doing your first collaboration can be scary. What if it doesn't get any views? What if your video is just awkward? Of course, there's always that possibility, but you'll never know until you try. Plus, collaboration gets easier with experience.

Great, so collaborations sound like an awesome way to grow my channel, but how do you find people to collaborate with, in the first place?

How to find collaborations

Finding collaboration partners when you first start your channel can certainly be tough. The key is developing organic relationships with other YouTubers in your genre.

Networking

First and foremost, YouTube is a social platform,

which means you always have to be networking in order to create and sustain relationships. This involves commenting on other YouTubers' channels and videos, giving people shoutouts in your own videos, retweeting other YouTubers on Twitter, following other YouTubers on Instagram, etc. Networking on YouTube is something that must be done daily if you want to see real results.

Reaching Out

Sometimes, it's just a matter of reaching out — if you find another YouTuber who lives in your city or state, or if you are traveling near their location, email them or leave them a comment explaining your idea for a collaboration. Even if you're not located near any other creators, you could try a remote collaboration. For example, you could try splicing some of their footage into your video, doing a tandem challenge video, a Q & A, or any other idea that relates to both of your channels.

Finding a YouTuber's email address is pretty easy — it's usually listed in their about section under contact info.

Focus on Similar Size Channels

Of course, it would be great to have 1,000 subscribers and collaborate with someone with 10,000, but it's not very realistic. There's just not much benefit for the other channel. The perfect collaboration is when there's something to be gained by both parties, so shoot for collaborating with channels close to your own subscriber count or view rate.

As you grow, the gap between subscribers becomes less consequential. For example, once you're at 10,000 subscribers, you might be able to collaborate with someone who has 20,000 subscribers. And once you're at 100,000, you might be able to collaborate with someone with 1 million!

Use Channel Pages

Channel Pages is a site where you can post your own channel and other YouTubers can connect with you in order to organize potential collaborations. Brands and agencies can also browse profiles there in order to find partnerships, so it might even help you make some money!

YouTube Advertising

You can earn an income just by making and uploading YouTube videos. YouTube runs ads on your videos and pays you a percentage of what they make. This is usually the first income stream that new YouTubers pursue. It's definitely the easiest and possibly the fastest.

We've all heard stories of people getting rich from their YouTube channels, but it's difficult to find out what people are actually earning through the platform. Those numbers we see online might be exciting if you're just starting out and have a low overhead. But when you factor in the incredible amount of time and work that goes into creating a show and building an audience, these numbers are really low. This is why I never recommend starting a YouTube channel primarily as a way to make money.

The YouTube ad system is driven by the concept of CPM. CPM stands for Cost Per Mile, which roughly translates to cost per thousand views. Individual views aren't worth much, but advertisers are willing to pay for them in batches of a thousand. It's really what makes the whole YouTube ecosystem work. If you have a mega-channel, you can do pretty well with this. But, unless your videos are generating hundreds of thousands of views on a regular basis, it's going to be difficult to scale this income stream up to something you can make a decent living on.

If you're familiar with Google's AdSense system, you'll have an idea of how the YouTube Ad system works. The majority of it actually is Adsense. Advertisers set up campaigns targeting certain keywords, interests, and demographics and place bids (auction-style) for ad placements. Some keywords are very competitive and can cost quite a bit.

Why Is CPM Great for Advertisers and Lousy for Creators?

Let's break down how CPM works. Say there's a hypothetical "How To Fly A Kite" video that has been on YouTube for over a month with, say, 10,000 views. Since it's a new channel and an average search term, if you're lucky, you might get a $5 CPM.

So 10,000 views/1,000 = 10 x $5 = $50.

Pretty sweet, right? Well, hold on a second. It never quite works out that way. You need to take one thing into account before you can make any type of projection — not all views are monetizable.

Non-monetized views don't count. You can find out which views actually count by going into your YouTube Analytics and clicking on Ad Performance. The Estimated Monetized Playbacks is the number that counts.

YouTube defines it as: "When a viewer views your video (i.e., a View) and is shown at least one ad impression, or when the viewer quits watching during the pre-roll ad without ever reaching your video."

10,000 − 5,000 = 5,000 views/1,000 = 5 x $5 = $25

And, of course, YouTube is going to take a cut — their payment for hosting the video and maintaining the system that makes this whole thing possible. Officially, that cut is 45%.

10,000 – 5,000 = 5000 views/1,000 = 5 x $5 = $25 - $11.25 = $13.75

These numbers are purely speculative, but it should give you an idea of how it works. After you take out the non-monetized Playbacks and then take out YouTube's percentage, the CPM that actually goes into your pocket is pretty low.

The part that can be discouraging is that (unless you have a viral smash) it takes a long time and a lot of work to make a significant income. This is a long-term play.

Once you start to hit a good number of views, everything looks a little bit different. You have money to reinvest into the business, and there's a sense of validation that comes with it. So, even though building a decent revenue stream through YouTube takes a lot of work and time, there are benefits above and beyond just the income. Use your YouTube earning numbers as a way to set goals, push yourself further, and make your channel better.

Conclusion

The purpose of social media is to make your brand familiar to people who have never even heard of it before. This takes a lot of time, so don't be disheartened if there aren't instant results. Social media requires dedication, patience, and effort. Your main goal should be to increase your audience as quickly as possible. Once you have achieved that, give them a reason to stay – engage with them by learning from them.

The biggest mistake people make is forgetting to take user feedback. People want to be heard and they like brands that care about what they have to say. So, communicate with your audience, and use social media to do exactly what it was meant for.

Once again, thank you for choosing this book. I hope you learned everything that you needed to know about social media in 2019.

References

15 LinkedIn Marketing Hacks to Grow Your Business. (2019). Retrieved from https://www.businessnewsdaily.com/7206-linkedin-marketing-business.html

Brenner, C. (2019). What is Instagram Marketing? (+7 Instagram Posts That Perform). Retrieved from https://learn.g2.com/instagram-marketing

Cronin, N. (2019). A Guide To Social Media Marketing For Business in 2019. Retrieved from https://www.hopperhq.com/blog/social-media-marketing-business-guide-2019/

DeMers, J. (2019). The Definitive Guide To Marketing Your Business On Facebook. Retrieved from https://www.forbes.com/sites/jaysondemers/2015/08/20/the-definitive-guide-to-marketing-your-business-on-facebook/#48986e1d2f51

DeStefano, B. (2019). How to Use LinkedIn as a B2B Marketing Tool: 4 Tips | SVM E-Marketing Solutions. Retrieved from https://www.svmsolutions.com/blog/how-use-linkedin-b2b-marketing-tool-4-tips

Facebook Marketing | What is Facebook Marketing?. (2019). Retrieved https://www.marketing-schools.org/types-of-marketing/facebook-marketing.html

Gotter, A. (2017). YouTube Marketing | A Complete Beginner's Guide. Retrieved from https://adespresso.com/blog/youtube-marketing/

Harris, J. (2019). Instagram Marketing: Social Media Experts Share Top Tips. Retrieved from https://contentmarketinginstitute.com/2019/03/instagram-marketing-experts/

Instagram Marketing: The Definitive Guide (2019). (2019). Retrieved from https://later.com/instagram-marketing/

Litza, T. (2018). 12 social media marketing trends to follow in 2019 - The Startup - Medium. Retrieved from https://medium.com/swlh/12-social-media-marketing-trends-to-follow-in-2019-af2749d8019e

Newberry, C. (2018). LinkedIn for Business: The Ultimate Marketing Guide. Retrieved from https://blog.hootsuite.com/linkedin-for-business/

Newberry, C. (2018). Facebook Marketing: A Step-by-Step Guide for Business. Retrieved from https://blog.hootsuite.com/facebook-marketing-tips/

Social Media Trends Report 2019. (2019). Retrieved from https://hootsuite.com/resources/social-media-trends-report-2019

The Beginner's Guide to YouTube Marketing for Small Businesses. (2019). Retrieved from https://www.wordstream.com/blog/ws/2018/09/20/youtube-marketing

www.ingramcontent.com/pod-product-compliance
Lightning Source LLC
Chambersburg PA
CBHW071736080526
44588CB00013B/2049